T0153011

THE ANIMAL

ONE THOUSAND MILES LONG

Seven Lengths of Vermont and Other Adventures

LEATH TONINO

TRINITY UNIVERSITY PRESS
San Antonio

For my parents

Published by Trinity University Press
San Antonio, Texas 78212

Copyright © 2018 by Leath Tonino

Book design by BookMatters, Berkeley
Cover design by Rebecca Lown

ISBN 978-1-59534-858-6 paperback
ISBN 978-1-59534-859-3 ebook

Trinity University Press strives to produce its books using methods and materials in an environmentally sensitive manner. We favor working with manufacturers that practice sustainable management of all natural resources, produce paper using recycled stock, and manage forests with the best possible practices for people, biodiversity, and sustainability. The press is a member of the Green Press Initiative, a nonprofit program dedicated to supporting publishers in their efforts to reduce their impacts on endangered forests, climate change, and forest-dependent communities.

The paper used in this publication meets the minimum requirements of the American National Standard for Information Sciences—Permanence of Paper for Printed Library Materials, ansi 39.48–1992.

CIP data on file at the Library of Congress

22   21   20   19   18 | 5   4   3   2   1

Printed in Canada

Contents

To know the spirit of a place is to realize that you are a part of a part and that the whole is made of parts, each of which is whole.

—GARY SNYDER,
The Practice of the Wild

We lose the sense of its unity and wholeness as we look it over; imagine, for instance, an animal a thousand miles long.

—ARISTOTLE, *Poetics*

Wilderness at Home

A game I often play goes something like this: I take the state of Vermont, grab it from both sides, one hand on the Connecticut River, the other on Lake Champlain, and pull, stretching it out flat, all the mountains and hollows and crinkles and rumples going smooth, right there before my eyes. Then I run my forearm along its length, back and forth, once, twice, three times, making it smoother still. I step away and survey my work. I see that this state—so small, so famously small—is quite huge. Seeing this, I'm reminded of my belief in the inexhaustibility of home, how what seems finite is actually, if not infinite, at least very large indeed. And I'm reminded, too, of how I came to this belief: by bushwhacking and camping and exploring along the spine of the Green Mountains for the better part of two decades, boots on the ground, sore feet, a smile on my face.

When President Lyndon Johnson signed the Wilderness Act in 1964, he set aside 9.1 million acres, nearly all of them west of the 100th meridian. John Muir's clean white Sierran granite, the Colorado Plateau's orange slickrock, the Pacific's turquoise shore—these are the colors our country wanted to protect and, accordingly, the colors we've commemorated with our glossy calendars ever since. A New England calendar? You know the type. There's always a barn in the corner of the shot, a dirt road winding this way or that, a row of apple trees, an orchard ladder leaning against some gnarled trunk. I can hear the voices in my head: oh, sure, Vermont is quaint, cute as a button, we love the cheese, but it can't possibly have any room for *true* wilderness. Too many villages, too much history. Ain't no Yellowstone, ain't no Alaska.

It's an issue of purity—the Purity Debate. Roderick Frazier Nash, in his 1967 classic of conservation history, *Wilderness and the American Mind*, writes: "There is the problem of how wild a region must be to qualify as wilderness, or, conversely, how much of the influence of civilization can be admitted. To insist on absolute purity could conceivably result in wilderness being only that land which the foot of man has never trod." The original '64 act defined wilderness narrowly, emphasizing the absence of humankind and human works. Nash goes on: "The question is one of degree. Does the presence of Indians or range cattle disqualify an area? Does an empty beer can? How about airplanes overhead?" (It's worth mentioning that there are only a dozen or so locations in the United States where a soundscape enthusiast can escape anthropogenic noise for a sustained fifteen-minute stretch, and that in the national parks, during daytime hours, the average spell of "silence" lasts a mere five minutes.)

Vermont was aggressively cut over back in the 1800s, the hills farmed and grazed and eventually abandoned when the soil eroded away. Between 1791 and the War of 1812, believe it or not, this state had the fastest-growing population of any in the Union. Go into the woods and you'll find the boomtime's traces: stone walls, stumps, cellar holes gathering leaves, a cable twisting snakelike through the duff. But here's the thing—you'll *barely* find these traces. What you're more likely to find on a hike in the Green Mountains is the exuberant growth that has overtaken and all but erased the signs of our species' long presence. You'll find the green. You'll swim through it. It will fill your ears with the whisper of wind in leaves, a whisper that is the voice of the land speaking its ancient inclination, a whisper that sounds like nothing so much as *trees, trees, trees, trees, trees, trees.*

"A place is wild when its order is created according to its own principles of organization—when it is self-willed land." So writes Jack Turner, an environmental philosopher and professional mountain guide from the Tetons in Wyoming. He's making an important distinction, a distinction between wilderness and wildness, between a thing (a zone on a map) and a quality (autonomy). Holding this distinction in our minds, we can expand understanding—grab it by the margins and stretch it out to make it larger, as it were, like smoothing our brains' mountain ranges to find extra room among the folds. Wilderness is not about being "untrammeled" or "primeval," as the '64 act would have it. Rather, wilderness is about *a process that is wild.* It's about the places where that process flourishes. It's about letting the land be the land, no questions asked.

In 1975, largely as a result of efforts made by George

Aiken, a senator from Vermont, Congress got the message and passed the Eastern Wilderness Areas Act; then, in 1984, it passed the Vermont Wilderness Act; then, in 2006, it passed the New England Wilderness Act. Today there are eight official wilderness areas in the Green Mountain National Forest: the Big Branch, the Breadloaf, the Bristol Cliffs, the George D. Aiken, the Glastenbury, the Joseph Battell, the Lye Brook, and the Peru Peak. They represent the wildness of a land in recovery, the flow of wildness across time, into the future. Hiking the 273-mile Long Trail, which traverses most of these areas, you will come upon primitive shelters and the occasional ramshackle privy, a lot of yellow birch and mountain ash and hemlock, a ton of funky lichens, and uncountable moose pellets. Maybe you'll find some faint memory of the pioneers who claimed the rugged uplands as home. *Maybe.*

⸪ ⸪ ⸪

During a recent camping trip in the Breadloaf, somewhere near the center of its 24,924 acres—acres that permit no chainsaws, bicycles, livestock, or car alarms—I stopped short on the trail. An eastern newt in its terrestrial phase (called a red eft) was crossing the moss that edged the dark mud, the dark mud that for hours had been squishing and squelching beneath my boots. The newt was less red than orange, so wet and vibrant it appeared as if freshly painted. I lowered to all fours, zoomed in, focused, and in a flash entered the microtopography, the earth's elaborate surface maze.

The meticulous nature appreciator Edward Hoagland, who for many decades has lived half the year in the Northeast Kingdom in an old farmhouse without electricity or telephone, writes: "Deer, otter, foxes are messengers from another condition of life, another mentality, and bring us tidings of places we don't go." The late Charles Bowden, of the Sonoran Desert, describes in hard, spare prose his attempts to enter "the kingdom of other bloods," meaning something like the consciousness of nonhuman species, rattlesnakes in particular. Barry Lopez, in *Arctic Dreams,* borrows the German term *Umwelt* from the biologist Jakob von Uexkull: "The world we perceive around an animal is its *environment*; what it sees is its *Umwelt*, or self-world. A specific environment contains many *Umwelten*, no two of which are the same."

I mention these lines in connection to the newt because, like my flattening-of-the-mountains game, they point toward another way of coming to appreciate the hidden vastness of Vermont's wilderness areas. Down there on my hands and knees, nose-close, the first thought that came to me was an old thought, really more of a personal fantasy I've been carrying in my daypack, next to gorp and raincoat, since my earliest childhood hikes: I would like to follow this newt; I would like to join this inching, participate in this adventure, crawl into the great forest fastness, through the Christmas ferns, over braided roots and slabs of polished schist, in and out of moist shadows and drying sun, away from the trail. A newt-guide! A newt-lens! For as long as I can remember, this has been my idea of ultimate fun.

Etymologically, the word "wilderness" derives from the Old English "wildeor"—the place of wild beasts. (Roderick Frazier Nash again: "One of the earliest uses was in the eighth-century epic *Beowulf*, where wildeor appeared in reference to savage and fantastic beasts inhabiting a dismal region of forests, crags, and cliffs.") Charles Johnson's *The Nature of Vermont*, published in 1998, tells us that we've got 54 species of mammals, 254 species of birds, 21 amphibians, 19 reptiles, and something like 20,000 insects inhabiting the state's various ecosystems. That's a lot of *Umwelten*, a real diversity of wild beasts. What would it look like, I wonder, to grab those styles of being and stretch them out flat? How far would that map extend?

My point is simple. Though animals' subjective realities will always be opaque to us, I take their very existence as an invitation, an opportunity to rub my *Umwelt* up against *Umwelten* not my own, to expand myself and my home by imagining. In the Breadloaf, as in the other wilderness areas (and much nondesignated countryside), the creatures who are our neighbors live wildly, autonomously, under their own control, according to their own design. And the same can be said of plants. Johnson estimates there are nearly two thousand species of angiosperms and between five thousand and fifteen thousand types of fungi in Vermont. The Green Mountains aren't the Grand Canyon, but to walk their length—to make a transect of so many lives—strikes me as a journey no less epic than a three-week float-trip on the Colorado River.

⁑ ⁑ ⁑

So far I've been using the metaphor of breadth, of surface area, to get at the inexhaustibility of place, but the notion of depth works just as well. In *Reading the Mountains of Home*, John Elder, a retired professor of English from Middlebury College, describes how by pairing his study of Robert Frost's poetry with countless hikes in the Bristol Cliffs Wilderness, he "gradually became aware of the natural, historical, and aesthetic *thickness* of the landscape." In an interview I conducted with Elder, he went on to explain that the ecology, pioneer history, and literary traditions of the local woods are, to his ear, three tones forming a harmony—a layered, symphonic texture rewarding those who listen close, who dig in. "I continue to discover more and more within a smaller and smaller radius of home," he said. It's a nice image, the circle contracting while the ground underfoot deepens.

Less than 5 percent of the nation's total designated wilderness (approximately 109 million acres) lies east of the Mississippi River, and only a fraction of that fraction can be found in New England. From one angle, this is troubling information, especially when paired with the statistic that the Green Mountain National Forest is located within an easy day's drive of 70 million people. Do the math and you'll come up with overcrowding, with a trampled, love-stunned wilderness that suffers from far worse than noise pollution and the occasional empty beer can. You'll likely retreat into the traditional and too-easy belief that nothing

but the Wild West, the Big Empty, the Glossy Nature Calendar, can provide the space necessary to teach us that—
borrowing words from David Brower, pioneering environmental activist—"civilization is only a thin veneer over the
deep evolutionary flow of things."

But wait a second: that's the wrong type of math. There's
a system of measurement that does not rely on acres and
miles, a kind of scraggly Vermont arithmetic with its own set
of rules. When you play by these new rules, applying them
to the Green Mountains, things get big again. The map is in
fact elastic. It stretches and stretches and stretches.

Such stretching returns us to the Breadloaf, to a newt
walking with the perfect steady slowness that is so becoming of newts, each movement like a breath, like a meditation, intentional and easy. I followed, practically on my
belly, my backpack catching on low branches, my attention
fixed. Step, step—a curled leaf made a tube. Step, step—
the newt entered one end of the tube. I waited for seconds
that felt like minutes and a minute that felt like an hour. I
waited. And waited. And then, finally, leveling my eye to
the ground for a peek inside, I saw what I could not believe.

The newt was gone, vanished, escaped by some secret
route, swallowed by some magical portal.

In a way, it made perfect sense. In a way, I followed.

Green Ghost Town

The year was 1761 and the governor of New Hampshire, Benning Wentworth, was on a spree. In a single day, sight unseen, he chartered six towns in the region that three decades later would be declared the state of Vermont. "But a governor who signed a sheepskin charter created neither population nor settlement," writes Tyler Resch in his book *Glastenbury: The History of a Vermont Ghost Town*. "When he chartered those towns, Benning had no idea what their topography was like. All he did was draw lines on paper, give names to the resulting squares (mostly of six miles per side) and sign documents he hoped would be taken seriously."

As it turned out, the topography in Benning's squares was—surprise, surprise—phenomenally rugged, rock-choked, densely forested. Homesteading in the Green Mountains' southern hollows was an uphill battle where "uphill" literally meant *uphill*, the growing season pinched by deep shade and lingering frost. For a short while, though, and against the odds, the town on the map named "Glossenbury" (the original British pronunciation) looked as if it just might amount to something more than a frisky governor's half-baked dream. In 1791 the population was 34; in 1860 it had grown to 47; in 1880 it hit a high of 241. There was a school, a post office, even singing and dancing on occasion. And then, abruptly, the dream broke apart. "Trees always provided the economy," writes Resch, "and when the trees were mostly gone, so were the settlements."

This story is hardly new. Its title is Profit and its main chapters are Resource Extraction, Shortsightedness, Ecological Collapse, and Abandonment. Don't get me wrong, I'm not knocking the individual characters, those tenacious pioneers who struggled to carve a life from the less-than-hospitable woods. It's just that these would-be Glastenburians, well, they carved too aggressively. A saw-mill at "the Forks" of Bolles Brook, where the village of South Glastenbury was located, turned out a thousand board feet an hour. Twenty-one massive brick kilns used in the manufacture of charcoal lined the valley bottom, each requiring a whopping forty to fifty cords of wood a day. In the frenzy of post–Civil War industrialization, the mountains were savagely clear-cut, the high terrain eroded away, and the earth lost its capacity to hold a heavy rain. When the infamous "freshet of '98" tore things up beyond repair (most devastatingly the eight-mile-long railroad line used to move freight to Bennington), it marked the end of a town that probably never should have been a town.

Here's to hoping, eh, Benning?

⸭ ⸭ ⸭

Today Glastenbury is home to two year-round families, a handful of seasonal residents, and who knows how many bears, birds, squirrels, moose, deer, snakes, and toads. One of five unincorporated towns in the state (neighboring Somerset is another), its population is too small to merit, let alone sustain, a local government with elected officers. Of its roughly twenty-seven thousand acres, the Green Mountain National Forest owns twenty-six thousand, the bulk of these managed as a federally designated wilderness area. "Especially in today's overpopulated and overscheduled North American civilization, there is an undeniable fascination with Glastenbury—a place that is definitely low-key and nontechnological," writes Resch. "Many find that just the knowledge that Glastenbury exists offers respite and even perhaps a touch of fantasy."

The first time I set foot in Glastenbury I was hiking on the Long Trail with three friends—and I was suffering. We were sixteen-year-olds, novice backpackers, and what had started with "a touch of fantasy" was suddenly very, very real. On the summit of Glastenbury Mountain, we climbed a steel lookout tower built in the 1920s and draped ourselves over railings at the top. Whether it was the exhaustion, the fact that we hadn't caught a glimpse outside the claustrophobic woods since leaving the Massachusetts border forty-eight hours earlier, or the inherent power of the scene itself, I'm unsure; all I can say for certain is that the panorama was staggering, almost hallucinatory. An ocean of trees. A dozen peaks over three thousand feet tall. Clouds moving like schools of fish across a vast upland so unlike the narrow, northern Green Mountains. I didn't know that this was, officially, the largest unsettled, roadless tract in Vermont, nor did I need to. It was so blatantly remote.

Last summer, twelve years after that initial encounter, I revisited Glastenbury with my dad for a little poking around. Driving south on Route 7, the Valley of Vermont's lush, tangled slopes struck me as a revelation. I had been out of the state for a number of months, working and traveling in the parched, sepia-toned West, and through fresh eyes I was seeing my home for what it really is: a place that grows and grows. Damn, I thought, this place really grows! I was excited, manic, overwhelmed, as if the Green Mountains' great green life force could at any moment surge up from beneath the pavement and smother the car with chlorophyll.

At Bennington we swung onto Route 9, ascended east, then swung onto Harbour Road, following it until the potholes were too deep to handle. Was this right? Hard to say. I walked a quarter of a mile to a house surrounded by horses and trucks and sheds, everything a bit crooked (equines included) and gave the door a couple of knocks. It took a while for somebody to come around, but eventually a man in a camouflage T-shirt and dirty baseball cap opened up. "Name's Ray. Been here for decades. Hunted the whole basin out back." I asked about the extinct village of South Glastenbury, hoping for hints, maybe even tips. Ray just sort of stared. "Years ago my neighbor pulled a bunch of bricks from the old dance hall chimney," he said at last. "Laid them out or did something with them." Another long stare. "Doubt you're going to see much up there."

Now, if you're anything like me, when you think "ghost

town" you think gold mines, saloons, dusty streets where time has been paused and buildings stand much as they did 150 years ago, albeit slightly worse for wear. To think this way in Vermont, though, is incorrect. Recall the Resch quote: *When the trees were mostly gone, so were the settlements.* As Ray knew, and as my dad and I would soon find out, it wasn't only the people that hightailed it from the hills; it was the structures, too. Log cabins, bridges, the company store, the school with its cute cupola—everything was swallowed, pulled groundward, eaten away by rot only to be built up again in the shape of new trees. Rain, decay, regeneration. If Colorado ghosts haunt mine shafts, New England ghosts haunt the very leaves.

Arriving at "the Forks" of Bolles Brook after an hour's hike on the Bennington & Glastenbury Railroad right-of-way (the tracks were pulled for scrap metal in World War II, and all that remains is a stony path), it was unclear whether we had reached our destination or just some random spot in the middle of the big woods. We spun circles, scanning for signs. A hundred hues—hunter, army, jade, shamrock, seaweed, parakeet—knit themselves around us, greens so vibrant they weren't colors but energies, moods. There's that life force again, I thought, a tingle zipping the length of my backbone.

My dad wandered off, disappearing behind tree trunks, leaving me by the quick water with Resch's book. I took a seat on a boulder and flipped to a black-and-white photograph of a denuded landscape scattered with slash and castaway planks, the smoke from a bonfire wisping up in one corner. The loggers' boardinghouse, three stories tall and 137 feet long, loomed over the brook in the foreground. *This* brook. *This* place. Men wearing hats. Men staring. Men wearing coveralls and jackets. Men in a line, squinting out at me. I closed the book and tried to imagine myself into the history—but couldn't, not immediately.

Time traveling, interestingly enough, takes time; to slip through the keyhole of the present into the enormity of the past requires a loosening of the mind, a relaxing of the part of ourselves that insists we are the center of everything, that insists the way it is today is the way it has always been and will forever be. What, then, to do? How to make the transition? Easy. Sit on the rock, feel the sun on your neck and the backs of your hands, listen to the noisy water at your feet. Relax. And once you've relaxed, go find those bits and pieces, those scraps of human stories that the erasing land has not entirely erased.

A rusty steel plate. A tumbled wall. An earthwork berm slumping under moss. Over the course of three hours— hours stumbling and crouching and inspecting, hours getting disoriented and returning to the brook to rest and read before pushing back into the thickets for further discovery—I did manage to ramble backward in time, if not all the way to the 1800s, then at least to some odd limbo between now and then. Stepping into a cellar hole, I sensed the invisible building above me. Leaning against a stout maple, I felt it shrink back to a sapling. Our archeological finds were mostly subtle, the traces faint, but the images they conjured were vivid, like movies in my head. I saw the woodcutter who died when he slipped on ice and his loaded oxcart crushed him. I saw teams of laborers feeding a kiln's maw, their faces streaked with soot. I saw the schoolmarm, the Swedish immigrants laying track for the train, the snow falling, the rain falling, the freshet ripping this valley to pieces.

The afternoon was subdued. Dull gold light slanted through the canopy's chinks. My dad's green shirt—the forest's 101st hue—kept appearing and vanishing, appearing and vanishing. We didn't talk much, just signaled with a nod or an outstretched arm to take note of this or that. Speech would have only drawn us away from the timelessness we'd partially achieved.

‡ ‡ ‡

On the final page of Resch's book, having led his reader from Benning Wentworth through decades of hardscrabble pioneering to the collapse, regeneration, and eventual acquisition of Glastenbury by the Forest Service, he asks, quite fairly: "Why is all this important?" There are, of course, many answers, and anybody who has bushwhacked into the forgotten recesses of the Green Mountains will have some unique contributions. For what it's worth, I find value in the haunting, by which I do not mean Halloween-style ghosts or spirits, but the stacking of stories in the earth underfoot. A haunt is a habitat, a place that an animal calls home. To have a home is to live in and with the stories of place. Inside Vermont, it is to search them out among the growing green.

A rusty steel plate. A tumbled wall. An earthwork berm slumping under moss. Something caught my eye and I stopped. It was a brick, a fuzzy, living, lichened brick already on its way to soil—part human, part forest, part present, part past. The charcoal kilns, I remembered, were 15 feet tall, 30 feet across, and built of 36,000 bricks. Twenty-one kilns, 756,000 bricks total. I began to dig and, one after another, the bricks emerged. Strata of bricks beneath me. Blankets of bricks twisted with roots, sifting the humus. A secret world of bricks where bugs and worms and threads of fungus roam.

Sizing up my pile, I heard Ray: *Doubt you're going to see much up there.* I could have dug on endlessly, or so it seemed.

On Track

Myles Ricketts is walking the track, "making the train." That's railroad speak for manually coupling the cars, a sort of industrial, workingman's version of linking daisies into a chain. Today's train will be made of fifteen fuel tankers and one empty limestone hopper. The tankers each hold twenty-five thousand gallons; the limestone hopper weighs 30 tons (130 tons when full). Put all sixteen cars together, add two engines—one in the back, the other up front—and you get a vehicle 1,080 feet long. That's longer than the Eiffel Tower is tall. That's ten basketball courts arranged end-to-end with a bowling lane pinned on for a caboose.

It's an hour after dawn, a summer morning that I assume is loud with insects and birds, though I can't be certain. Steve Dike and I are sitting in the high, noisy cab of Vermont Rail System Engine 311—the lead engine—layers of hum and drum, rumble and hiss, not just in our ears but vibrating up through our stools, into our backsides. We're idling at milepost 56, near the north end of the Rutland yard. Milepost 120, the Burlington yard, will be our destination.

Steve is the engineer; he's responsible for driving the train. Myles, the conductor, takes care of on-the-ground details and paperwork: track warrants, shifting lists, hazmat bills. A young guy with steel-toed boots, a round face, and a scraggly beard, he's only been on the job for eight months. Steve, a veteran, has worked this section of line in various capacities for twenty-seven years.

I ask about the limestone. "It's in everything," Steve says. "They put it in paper to make it white. They put it in toothpaste. They put it in paints and plastics. If it's out there, it's probably got limestone in it." There's a plant in Florence, a town we'll be passing through shortly, that processes crude rock into calcium carbonate slurry. Steve makes a fist to indicate the size of the cobbles that fill the hoppers he regularly hauls to the plant. He says he hauls tankers full of slurry, too.

Steve's fist. It's smudged with dark grease and connected to a forearm thicker than my thigh. He's a huge man, a train of a man, a 3,000-horsepower engine just like the 311, though instead of bold red paint he's got whitening hair, jean shorts, and a navy blue tank top. Seated before a console of gauges and levers the approximate dimensions of a refrigerator, he appears its equal.

The cab's walls and ceiling are dingy, stained with water and grime (the 311 was new in 1976). Eight smallish windows provide a 180-degree view, and though I've never been on the bridge of a ship, I'm reminded of one. Through the front windows I see the track extending out in a perfectly straight line, foliage on either side, forest canopy overhead. It's a chute, an arboreal tunnel.

Still waiting on Myles, I ask what other types of freight

get moved on this line. Steve answers with a list: plywood, fertilizer, Valero heating oil, lots of road salt, some propane, the occasional boxcar of wine bottles and barrels, flour for Westminster Cracker, soy and corn and other grains for Blue Seal Feeds and Feed Commodities and Bourdeau Brothers. Vermont Rail System runs a train from Rutland to Burlington and back seven days a week, 365 days a year. The track follows the Route 7 corridor and services the towns of Brandon, Leicester, Middlebury, Vergennes, and Shelburne, among others. I tell Steve that I live in Ferrisburgh and that if I turn my ear to the nearby woods I can hear, as Hank Williams would put it, "that lonesome whistle blow." He asks where *exactly* I live. Unfamiliar with the milepost, I describe other landmarks: a field, a rutted farm road, a place where the track begins a gradual leftward bend. "I know it," he says. "I shot a deer there years ago."

The train made, Myles climbs a narrow stairwell up into the cab, sits down beside me, and organizes his paperwork. Steve moves a lever. I'm expecting a full-throated "All aboard!" and a clanging bell—like something out of an old film—but it never comes. There's nobody to signal, no reason to clang. There's just an empty limestone hopper and a million gallons of fuel and the three of us. The green tunnel blurs on both sides. The trip will last five hours.

⁂ ⁂ ⁂

I want to say that a lot happens, but really it's like nothing much happens and all that nothing much, when considered en masse, somehow *feels* like a lot. Four crows swoop in front of the engine and are pushed along for a hundred feet on a pillow of air before rising out of the way. Marshy lowlands appear on the right and left; Steve mentions how during a flooding event the water once came up within a foot of the rails, making it feel like the train was running over the surface of a vast pond. Fog can pool around the train, he says, and slick leaves and deep snow, depending on the season, can make the going hard.

A cottontail rabbit bursts from the brush. A gray squirrel leaps. We repeatedly cross Otter Creek on low bridges without guardrails—our line straight, the creek sinuous, always doubling back. I point out some beaver-chewed stumps and am assured that, yes, the gosh-darn varmints frequently drop logs across the track. Myles seems more peeved about it than Steve. Maybe it's that Steve has worked on the line longer, has come to terms with the furry, big-toothed landscape architects. Or maybe it's that his son-in-law has a permit to trap beavers, so he feels avenged.

I'm excited to be along for the ride, excited to see the woodlots and grazing Holsteins of the Champlain Valley from a new angle. I tell the guys that it feels like I'm hopping a train without hopping one, which prompts Steve to roll his eyes. "They'll curl up in any tiny hole anywhere," he says of hoppers. "A month ago I looked out to check the cars on a curve and there was a guy sitting on top of the train." Usually Steve asks nicely: *It's not safe, will you please leave?* But sometimes a hopper will hop back on just as soon as the train gets moving again. That's when Steve calls the authorities.

Radios crackle to life intermittently during our travel, filling the cab with snippets of overheard conversation. The engine and clattery track noise make it hard to hear clearly, but I'm pretty confident somebody says, "Who's running that?" and another person, maybe in an office, answers, "Sparks and Chris J. And the other is Rockin' Rod." I assume they're talking of different trains on different lines, perhaps a crew routed to Bennington or Whitehall.

The tankers trailing behind us are destined for Burlington; there will be no intermediary stops on this run. At times we talk but mostly we stare, mesmerized by the streaming green tunnel, bored in a way that feels less boring than soothing. The engine sways dreamily from side to side, again reminding me of an ocean vessel. I ask about the swaying and receive a lecture on the differences between welded rail and stick rail, the latter characterized by cracks where two pieces of rail are joined together with angle bars. When the train's wheels chatter over these cracks, the chatter moves up through the body of the train, causing the sway. Sometimes it feels like the train will topple. Needless to say, it won't.

Most Vermont Rail System engines, I'm told, are geared to go as fast as 60 or 65 miles per hour, but on this trip we won't exceed 40, and sometimes we'll slow to 10 or 15. This surprises me. I'd assumed that with the track completely to ourselves we'd burn rubber or scorch steel or whatever. It turns out that trains, like cars, are subject to speed limits. Bad ties, bad rails, sinkholes—these demand caution. And in addition to official limits, there are physical limitations.

The steepest grade we'll climb this morning is three degrees, and even a one-degree slope can challenge the strength and stamina of three thousand horses. We are, after all, hauling the Eiffel Tower.

⁘ ⁘ ⁘

This is the stuff—the wonderful, banal stuff—of the 311's everyday: a man with a newspaper under his arm walking the scruffy edge of the Middlebury yard; a foothill ridge that takes on different shapes as it's seen from different angles; a farmer waving from his tractor; the occasional view west to the Adirondacks; the interplay of sun and shadow on the ground out front.

A pair of white-tailed deer, one on either side of the track, nibble at the green tunnel. Steve gives them a nod—just a pleasant wildlife sighting. Then, instantly, it feels dangerous, as if the doe on the right might not get out of our path, or might leap in the wrong direction. Seeing that soft brown body trembling with indecision, the power of the train—its sheer unstoppable bulk—sizzles into my cerebral cortex. Steve blows the whistle. He tenses ever so slightly. The doe springs and I'm positive we're going to collide and, *whew*, she's running with the other in a field of clover to our left.

"We don't see as many as we'd like," Steve says, which is a testament to his love of *Odocoileus virginianus*. Before eleven in the morning we've already had five encounters totaling nine animals: deer out in the open, deer disappearing in shrubbery, deer stotting past hay bales, deer standing still, deer studying the train. One of the perks of the job is that during hunting season Steve's allowed to bring his rifle. He points out a spot where he shot a deer right on the track. To me it resembles every other spot for miles in both directions, but not to him.

The rail line, in the minds of Myles and Steve, is mapped with anecdote and fact, overlays of memory and meaning. *My friend lives here…there's a wrecked car down that bank… a Ferrari mechanic works out of this garage…a windstorm knocked the roof off that barn while they were building it and the carpenters had to start all over again.* Myles highlights a hole where a culvert is washing out; he makes sure I see it, makes sure I know it's coming. The hole is a potential threat, but it's also *more* than a potential threat. It's a landmark, a milepost without a number. With the clarity of a street sign, it tells him where he is—a knowledge, some would claim, that trumps all else in significance.

For my part, I'm about as discombobulated as I've ever been in the Champlain Valley. Roads I've traveled for decades intersect the track at perpendicular angles, but I don't recognize them; seeing the world 90 degrees off normal has spun me dizzy. This is the land of my youth, land of ten thousand explorations on foot and in autos—this is the place I know better than any other—and here I am riding a train, not knowing it in the slightest. I mention my confusion, my whacked-out internal compass. "I used to take my kids on the train and I'd ask them which side of Route 7 they thought we were on," Steve says. "They hardly ever knew."

Passing through Ferrisburgh, despite my searching, I

can't identify the field that marks my neighborhood, the rutted farm road, the gradual leftward bend in the track. Two minutes too late, at an intersection where cars wait in a line behind a lowered gate and flashing red lights, I decipher our position. The driver in the front car is peering up at us. His is a perspective to which I can relate; it's how I've always encountered the trains of my home, at least until this morning.

Steve gives a nod—the same nod he greeted the two does with—and blows the whistle. The man nods back. Then we're in the tunnel again, right on schedule, right on track, mesmerized by the green blur and, in my case, totally happily lost.

Bumping Into Life

Chris O'Donnell has walked to Egypt. She's also been moved to tears in Charleston, camped solo on the shore of Maidstone Lake, changed out of her wet bathing suit in a Rutland parking lot, and all but bumped into a brown wall of moose-flank on a trail in Nebraska Notch (whereas in Ripton she only stood ankle-deep in pellets). Riding her bicycle on Route 30 in Whiting one Sunday morning, she passed a church where gospel singers from South Carolina were performing, a general store with two dozen long-bearded Harley Davidson dudes revving out front, and a massive yard sale. Cemeteries, quarries, and streambeds across the state have registered her bootprint; Hard Rock Mountain in Sheffield has felt the bite of her snowshoes' teeth. And then there's the hot dog at the baseball game in Canaan that was the tastiest ever, and the gunshots in Underhill.

She chuckles. "Every one of these trips is an adventure. They're all that perfect blend of planning and spontaneity. It's like jazz, like my teaching—there's freedom in structure."

Chris and I are sitting at a circular table in her classroom at Champlain Valley Union High School in Hinesburg, both of us leaning in, tracing our fingers over a *Vermont Atlas and Gazetteer*. At first glance it seems just like any other: a little creased, a little worn from use. The more maps we fan through, though, the more I come to appreciate the near-magical power they have to draw anecdotes and images—details—from the depths of memory. Each green and yellow page bears scratches of red ink, as if a child had been set loose during art class with a juicy pen. Towns are check-marked and circled. Roads are highlighted. Cryptic shorthand notes hide among topographic lines. Here a squiggle, there a squiggle—everywhere bits and pieces of journeys Chris has made.

For the past handful of years Chris has been on a mission to "do something outdoorsy" in each of Vermont's 251 towns. Mostly she travels alone ("I enjoy my own company") and manages to visit six or seven towns over the course of a weekend ("I say that I 'knock 'em off,' but I know that makes it sound like I'm robbing banks or something"). She swims, she hikes, she bikes, she paddles, she cross-country skis, she snowshoes, she mixes and matches. Some days it's a game of connect-the-dots, each dot a swimming hole or a hill with a view; other days it's a bike ride through one town to a trailhead in the next for a hike that leads to a mountaintop in a third. "I spend a lot of time looking at the places where town lines intersect," she says, searching her atlas for a good example. "Corners are usually unmarked and off in the middle of nowhere. They make for interesting outings."

I point to Barton.

"The big thing in the Northeast Kingdom is people gathering around pickup trucks. That's a get-together: standing around a pickup truck in the backyard, talking."

I point to Poultney.

"That was one of my best days. It was really hot and turned into swim, swim, swim, swim, swim. Lots of lakes and ponds, but don't think I'm going to tell you my favorite spot. That's a secret."

And Burlington?

"I came upon a bunch of North Enders in Ethan Allen Park, indigenous Africans in bright clothing. They were foraging, crouched down, sorting nuts and berries. I stopped and watched from a distance. It was absolutely unexpected and absolutely stunning to see this face of Vermont."

She pauses, leans back in her chair. "The spontaneity, the serendipity, that's what makes it so interesting for me. It's like bumping into life."

⁂

Aristotle claimed that philosophy is the loftiest of human activities precisely because it's useless: not a means to an end, but an end in itself. Though Chris doesn't reference the Greeks directly, it's pretty obvious this is how she conceives of her project. In 1954 Arthur Peach, a retired professor of English from Norwich University, founded the 251 Club, which today has 4,000-plus members. "I don't know much about that," Chris says. "Do they go to every post office and get a stamp or something?" Despite the bank robber talk and map marking, she's not all that interested in keeping a strict tally of her peregrinations. For her, a destination—

whether a creek or a village—is a springboard to the un-known. If her project is a means to anything, it's to engage-ment, to poking around.

Chris has taught history at Champlain Valley Union for almost four decades. I was a student of hers many years ago and remember fondly our third-period quests—Spring mud? Who cares!—for cellar holes and stone foundations in the swales beyond the school's soccer fields and baseball diamonds. "On a given day I don't know what I'm going to do," she says of her teaching style. "I want to make sure I'm not quite sure what's going to happen." Her hiking is simi-lar: "I'll just stop the car and crash into the woods anywhere at any time. I like to bushwhack. 'I'm not lost, I just don't know where I am right now'—that's sort of my mantra. The woods have always been a comfortable place for me, I guess."

Raised in rural northern Massachusetts, Chris has a sort of neighborly affection for earthy, freewheeling Transcen-dentalists like Emerson and Thoreau. As a child, when she wanted to visit a friend's house, she jumped on a forest path out back and walked. In high school, obsessed with bagging peaks, she made pilgrimages to the Northeast's four-thou-sand-footers. For a time she fantasized of backpacking the entire Appalachian Trail or end-to-ending the Long Trail, but such extended wilderness immersions don't easily jibe with career and family.

"After kids you've got less discretionary time," she says. "It's like, 'Okay, I dropped them off, I've got an hour, where can I go?'" Small outings became the norm—pulses and blips of exploration, miniadventures stuffed into the cracks between the weeks. But here's the delightful surprise: the landscape actually *expands* when you approach it this way.

Chris grins. "There are so many neat little things you can see and do once you step away from the classic hikes and give yourself more terrain to play with. There are so many options in every town."

◦ ◦ ◦

Now in her sixties, an outdoorsy 251 strikes Chris as more appropriate than ever. "I tell people it's a great geriatric project because it's all about moderation," she says. "My bike rides are only ten miles, and a lot of my hikes are just a quick stroll on a nature trail. If I start at six in the morning, by the end of the day I've gotten a ton of exercise and I haven't ruined my knees on some endless descent."

Her first outing was a thirteen-town tour of the Northeast Kingdom. Since, she's visited much of northern Vermont, including all of Franklin, Chittenden, and Lamoille Counties. Off the top of her head she doesn't know how many towns she has left to go ("Maybe I'm halfway there?"). I ask if she's got any special plans for the state's tight, hilly south and she says no, nothing in particular. And what about a grand finale? "I suppose I could end at home in Westford and have a party," she says. "Or maybe I could do each corner and then end in the middle, like an *X*." She pages through the maps, searching. "I think the middle is Randolph—does that sound right? I guess I'd have to figure that out first, huh?"

Having talked for a solid hour—and concerned that the *Atlas and Gazetteer*'s magical powers could transfix us for another—I suggest we get outside and stretch our legs. Chris offers to show me some trails a few miles away, a preserve she visits frequently during the school year, sneaking in strolls before or after classes, errands, and appointments. I mention that I was a pretty committed hiker during high school, getting out into the local foothills multiple times a week, but that I've never heard of these trails at the center of town, just behind the supermarket. "Exactly," she says. "I wasn't aware of them for a long time either. And they're right under our nose!"

It's a gorgeous, windows-down afternoon that energizes and makes tangible everything we've been discussing. Bobolinks sing from the power lines. The scent of cut hay thickens the air. Three minutes out from the high school, we pass a young couple with bulky backpacks walking on the side of the road. "I wonder where they're headed," Chris says, as anybody might. Then, without warning, she pulls over, as nobody would. "Why don't you hop out and ask? I'll wait for you up the road." The speed of the transition reminds me of an interview with Mary Oliver in which the poet talks about reducing the space between her ideas and actions, between *envisioning* something and *doing* it. Chris is like this—curious, snappy, unabashed in her pursuit of the moment.

So out the door I go, and fifty strides later I'm keeping pace with a guy named Sorya and a gal named Lida, talking about adventure and serendipity and openness and engaging home terrain and the deep joys of living in the Green Mountains. My new friends tell me that they're on a multiweek walking meditation, touring aimlessly around the state, and that they've done this every summer for a number of years. There are only two rules: keep to the roads (no backcountry) and never pay for lodging (no State Park campsites, no B&Bs). The restrictions are designed to keep them in the flow of people and place, to get them meeting strangers and strange circumstances. That I should spring from a random vehicle, chase them, and strike up a conversation is, in a way, exactly what they've been anticipating.

"You're bumping into life," I say, knowing that I am too.

Chris is waiting in a driveway not far off, leaning against the hood of her car, chewing a long green stem of grass. When we reach her I make introductions all around, hardly able to contain my excitement. The timing of this chance encounter seems impossibly perfect—yet here we are, standing in the sun, sharing stories like it's totally familiar.

"I'm in awe of this place," Chris says when we get back in the car, still chewing, the grass stem bobbing in front of her face. And with that we're moving, searching for a hike and whatever a hike will bring.

Seat Mountain

"Tundra is a word that describes an area, a kind of vegetation, and a specific ecosystem. It is a word that characterizes the land beyond treelimit, whether it be the marshy grasslands of the Arctic with permanently frozen soils, or the high alpine reaches." So writes Ann Zwinger in the opening pages of her book *Land above the Trees: A Guide to American Alpine Tundra*.

As a college freshman, I was lucky enough to take a class with Zwinger, a revered naturalist, artist, and author who was then in her early eighties. On a weeklong field trip she tramped at the front of our group, twisting her ankles in gopher holes, pricking her fingers on thorny bushes, hair perfectly coiffed, face framed by pearl earrings. To say she was one tough grandma would be an understatement. She was an inspiration. It was as though all the rugged, remote landscapes she'd explored over her long life were present inside her, their vital energies made her own.

More than Zwinger herself, though, what I remember is the advice she gave us students. I don't have the verbatim quote, but it went something like this: Find a place, a gully or a boulder or a tree, and spend as much time there as you can. Sleep there. Take your meals there. Hold yourself to the place. Get bored. Get tired. Get cold and confused. See it from countless angles. Notice everything. This is how you'll learn.

Which brings me back to tundra, specifically the ten-acre patch of tundra capping 4,083-foot Camel's Hump. What better spot to get bored, tired, cold, and confused than on the raw, rocky summit of Vermont's most prominent peak?

This past summer I did just that, hiking to a narrow ledge cutting the mountain's massive south-facing cliff. It's a perch I've visited many times over the years, in all seasons and weathers, usually alone. On this excursion the wind was relentless. Thin clouds ripped themselves to pieces across the sky, larger clouds behind them blocking out the afternoon sun. The route down to the ledge was damp and slippery, but with focus I managed the tricky moves and set-tled at my favorite seat.

Solitudo is the Latin word for "wilderness." Yes indeed. A wall rose at my back, twenty feet tall, cracked and blocky, stained with moisture. Beyond the soles of my boots there was nothing but gray: a gauzy swirl, a swirly gauze. I cinched my hood tight and recalled the Abenaki creation story told by Joseph Bruchac. "Gluskabe threw his leg over Camel's Hump and made it his seat, Dawabodiiwadzo (The Seat Mountain)."

Then I did the only thing left to do. I hunkered. Zwinger-style.

⁂

Writes Charles Johnson, longtime Vermont State Natural-ist: "Although true Arctic tundra is one of the largest veg-etation zones on the North American continent, the Arc-tic-like areas of Vermont should be considered endangered communities, since they are so uncommon here and almost all the plants are either threatened with extinction or else extremely rare." Besides the 10 acres on Camel's Hump, the only other tundra ecosystems in the Green Mountains are the 250-acre swath running north–south on Mt. Mansfield's main ridge and a stamp-sized yard on Mt. Abraham. That's it. In Zwinger's poetic words, these are "isolated areas of limited extent and unlimited fascination."

A comparison is often made between tundra peaks and islands, and it is apt. Picture the tallest mountain on earth, Hawaii's 33,474-foot Mauna Kea, the bulk of which is underwater. Underwater, underforest—it's basically the same idea. Oceans of conifers lap at the rugged shores of bald summits. Green swells ease off toward the Whites, toward the Adirondacks, toward archipelagos on far hori-zons. When foul conditions prevail above treeline, you can almost feel like a shipwrecked survivor.

But fitting as the analogy to islands might be, sitting on the Seat Mountain, waiting for nothing, it becomes clear that tundra is also a bridge, a way of connecting the finite here-and-now with a boundless past.

Fifteen thousand years ago, near the end of the Wis-consin Glacial Episode, ice covered New England. As the climate warmed, that ice retreated, melting northward, revealing a moonscape of polished, sculpted granite. In my imagination I go backpacking through this Vermont of pure stone. The terrain is surreal, pools of silver water winking with light, rippled by breeze. No life. No growth or breath. Just sunrise and sunset, subtle colors and textures, an austere and beautiful world.

Over the following millennia, vegetation crept across the region, ever so slowly blanketing the topography with tundra. Again, I dream myself into the scene. Herds of caribou and mammoths move like fluid across a broad lowland plain. Paleoindians give chase, spears at the ready. Spruce-fir forests encroach as the climate continues to warm, the treeless spaces shrinking, contracting around cooler heights. The tops of Dawabodiiwadzo and Mozondebiwadzo (Moose Head Mountain, aka Mt. Mansfield) become exotic gardens.

Today, alpine bilberry and mountain cranberry grow on gentle slopes. Bigelow's sedge and various alpine grasses make pads and cribs on harsher northern aspects. Three-toothed cinquefoil, mountain sandwort, and mountain firmoss anchor in crevices where gravels collect. These are the very species that felt the caribou's hoof and the mammoth's hot breath way back when.

Zwinger: "All tundra vegetation is more uniform in aspect and composition throughout its extent than any other major vegetation type on earth. The same plant species can be found growing in Lapland, the Alps, Alaska, or Colorado. The rolling, open, treeless landscape; the soil patterns caused by frost action; and the carpet of low plants can make an arctic or alpine ecologist feel remarkably at home, whether in Kamchatka, New Hampshire, India or California."

The summit of Camel's Hump isn't only a bridge to pre-history, then, but also a bridge to the far-flung present, to places with names like Svalbard and the Gulf of Ob. More than anything, though, it is a bridge to itself.

⁂

Two hours into my vigil the wind was still fierce, the clouds snapping like tattered, threadbare flags, the afternoon dimming, pressing in close. My mind had wandered through time and space, to the Ice Age and Siberia, and now it was back, firmly grounded in my body, my body grounded through my rear to the cold, hard, 500-million-year-old rock.

Teeth chattering, fingers red and stiff, I got up, stretched, and walked the length of the ledge. I sat back down. My nose dripped. I tucked my shirt into my pants and my pants into my socks. Another gust. Blustery, blustery. Nothing to do but hunker on.

I'd love to say that I'm a diligent naturalist, a geologist inspecting crystal formations with a hand lens, a botanist sketching heather in fine graphite lines, an entomologist keying out species of *Coleoptera* (a study of insect fauna conducted in 1870 on Camel's Hump found twenty-one species of beetles). Alas, I am none of these. What I am is a patient guy with limited scientific understanding and a willingness—no, an *eagerness*—to tough out the alpine zone's offerings.

The goal on my favorite ledge is always the same: no

goal, just sit. Aldo Leopold, pioneering ecologist and environmental ethicist, once wrote of "thinking like a mountain." Precisely. Think like chartreuse lichen. Think like a red-backed vole. Think like schist. Think slow, elemental thoughts until these thoughts drop from the head into the elbows, the knees, the hands, the toes. In other words, think like a mountain until you *feel* like a mountain, until you're not *thinking* at all.

In the ninth century, Chinese poet Po Chu-i spoke of mountains as "the perfect place to get free of your name." Po Chu-i was a Buddhist, so there are certainly overtones of enlightenment humming nearby—but on the whole, as with much of the best literature, the line is open to interpretation. For me it has something to do with Zwinger's advice and Leopold's imperative. In getting free of our names, we don't become *nobody*, we become *some place*.

§ § §

Hours, hours, more hours came and went, each blowing through me as though I were a door flung wide by the wind. At some point, a dark-eyed junco landed on a slab three feet to my left, tiny bird-feet ballasting the body's slight weight against bursts rushing up the cliff. For a moment the clouds released and a view down the chain of peaks opened: Ethan Allen, Lincoln, Bread Loaf, Killington. The sun was going, the sky pink and purple and delicate blue.

Soon it would be night. I had a headlamp in my pack and a sandwich for dinner. A bit longer, I told myself. A bit longer before beginning the descent.

Two months after this Camel's Hump vigil, at the age of eighty-nine, Ann Zwinger passed away, leaving behind more than a dozen books as well as generations of inspired students and readers. Hearing the news, I immediately, instinctively wanted to climb back to the secret ledge on Camel's Hump and sit again—not out of sadness, but out of gratitude. It was a busy week, though, and as is too frequently the case, an afternoon of quiet observation got nudged from the schedule by various commitments.

It's okay. The Seat Mountain is vivid within me, the tundra a part of myself, and that right there is homage to my former teacher and her special advice.

Eyes closed, watching, the junco hops toward the rim of the ledge. A lull. A touch of warmth. Then the gray swamps back in, hugging tight, and the bird shoots like a small, sharp arrow into the void. *Solitudo.* Here I am. Only the mountain for company.

Seeing Is an Art

You know Henry David Thoreau and you know John Muir and you know Teddy Roosevelt. You probably have heard of Aldo Leopold (*A Sand County Almanac*), Rachel Carson (*Silent Spring*), and Edward Abbey (*Desert Solitaire*). These are the famous nature lovers of American history, the writer-thinker-preachers we credit with opening our collective awareness to the glories of the wild. Dirt under their nails, wind in their hair, they taught us to go slow, listen close, rove and wonder and respect and protect and defend and cherish. We heap praise on them, and rightly so. They deserve it.

But what of George Perkins Marsh, born in 1801? Do you know his name? Outside that green tribe composed of environmental historians, ecophilosophers, professional conservationists, and rangers at the Marsh-Billings-Rockefeller National Historic Park, site of Marsh's childhood home in Woodstock, he doesn't get much play. Within that tribe, though, he's a prophet, a seer, a sage, and his book—*Man and Nature; or, Physical Geography as Modified by Human Action*—is a kind of bible.

Like any good book, *Man and Nature*, originally published in 1864 and reprinted many times since, comes loaded with blurbs. Lewis Mumford: "the fountainhead of the conservation movement." Gifford Pinchot: "epoch-making." Stewart Udall: "the beginning of land wisdom in this country." Wallace Stegner: "the rudest kick in the face that American initiative, optimism, and carelessness had yet received."

Marsh's biographer, David Lowenthal, ranks *Man and Nature* "the most influential text of its time next to Darwin's *On the Origin of Species*, published just five years earlier." In an introduction to a 2003 reprint, he summarizes the book's core argument: "Humans depend upon soil, plants, and animals. But exploiting them deranges and may devastate the whole supporting fabric of nature. To forestall such damage we need to learn how nature works and how we affect it. And then we must act in concert to retrieve a more viable world." The word "ecology" wasn't coined until 1866, two years after *Man and Nature* came out, but ecological collapse is precisely what's at stake.

Marsh speaks in a sterner language than his biographer, which is part of the fun of his book. A bespectacled polymath scholar with a pudgy face, a round belly, and a beard best described as ursine (black bear in the prime of his life, polar bear near the end), he warns the still-young American republic that "human crime and human improvidence" can reduce the earth "to such a condition of impoverished productiveness, of shattered surface, of climatic excess, as to threaten the deprivation, barbarism, and perhaps even extinction of the species." He uses the metaphor of a house:

We are tearing apart the dwelling we live in, ripping out the floors and doors and window frames to fuel the fire of our needs and wants. And, of course, the house can't easily be rebuilt. "Marsh was the first to recognize that man's environmental impacts were not only enormous and fearsome, but even cataclysmic and irreversible," writes Lowenthal. The book's proposed title, rejected by its publisher, was *Man the Disturber of Nature's Harmonies.*

Does any of this sound radical? Is it ear-catching, head-turning talk? By today's standards, what with every magazine article and TV report pushing doomsday scenarios in which runaway development, fossil fuel consumption, and population growth (to name a few) spell the end of rainforests, shoreline cities, and potable water (to name a few), no, this is hardly big news. But try to imagine encountering *Man and Nature*, all 465 vehement, erudite pages of it, at the moment of its publication. The website for the George Perkins Marsh Institute at Clark University offers some context: "The conventional idea held by geographers of the day, Arnold Guyot and Carl Ritter, was that the physical aspect of the earth was entirely the result of natural phenomena, mountains, rivers, oceans." In other words, humans were one thing, nature something else, and the former had no impact on the latter.

Lowenthal describes the middle of the nineteenth century as "the peak of Western resource optimism" and says that New England's pioneers were caught up in the myth of limitless plenty." Between 1791 and the War of 1812, Vermont was the fastest-growing state in the Union. By the

1850s it was almost entirely deforested, much of the lumber going to produce potash and charcoal that provided a cash bonus for the hill farmers doing the cutting. Come 1860, 42 percent of native-born Vermonters had "outmigrated" to places like the Ohio Valley—to the promise of Beyond and the assured abundance of Elsewhere.

Hindsight being hindsight, we can now see how the dots connect to form a line that sprints straight off a cliff. We can see the axes glinting and the trees toppling, the naked earth crumbling, the rainstorms tearing steep slopes to pieces. We can see the sediments clotting the rivers, the fish floating dead in pale-bellied rafts, the beaver, moose, and deer flickering out like ghosts. We can see thousands of sheep grazing gullied pastures, chewing the ground with their teeth and hooves. And we can see the men—earnest, industrious, well-intentioned, ignorant—their heads lowered to the task of unwittingly ruining the land.

The tallgrass prairie of Iowa was plowed under by 1876, the American bison an inch from extinction in 1890.

"Sight is a faculty," Marsh writes in *Man and Nature*, "seeing, an art."

⸭ ⸭ ⸭

How a country boy from Vermont grew up to revise—to re-vision—his culture's destructive attitudes and normalized practices is a story full of improbable, too-perfect alignments. It begins in 1808 with a seven-year-old Marsh hunched over an encyclopedia in a dim room in a Victorian mansion in Woodstock. He's a possessed reader, and after he has spent a week straight squinting at the pages, the words begin to blur away. His father, a wealthy lawyer, forbids further study, ordering his nearly blind son outside to heal in the light.

It takes many days for Marsh's eyesight to come back, and when it does it's as though he's seeing the natural world for the first time. An "interminable forest" rolls away in all directions, leafy canopy trembling overhead. The boy hikes. He roams. He learns the word "watershed," learns the ridges and valleys, the forces that shaped them, the rhyme and reason of the earth beneath his feet. According to the documentary *A Place in the Land*: "The plants and animals were persons" to him, "not things." Years later he'll fondly remember spending his early life "almost literally in the woods."

But the glinting axes—you know what the glinting axes do. By the time he's seventeen, heading off to Dartmouth College in New Hampshire, Marsh's home is fast becoming a scrapeland, a scabland, a scarland. The year is 1818. It's the height of the boom. Mt. Tom stands behind the family's house, a lump in a mosaic of stumps and rocky ledges. The Ottauquechee River floods its banks, heavy and brown, sanding over the meadows. These images enter Marsh and grab hold of something deep, never to let go.

Following his graduation from Dartmouth, Marsh's accomplishments pile up to form a sort of Renaissance man's résumé. A lawyer by training, he serves as Vermont railroad commissioner, fish commissioner, and State House commissioner, and is elected to four terms as representative in

Washington, DC, where he helps create the Smithsonian Institution and design the Washington Monument. Fluent in twenty languages, respected around the world as a premier linguist, he translates German verse, Danish law, and Swedish fiction. In addition to being intellectually brilliant, he remains a down-to-earth, practical-as-ever Yankee, dabbling in marble quarrying, woolen manufacturing, and farming. As Lowenthal puts it, his "omnicompetence was legendary."

And now things get really interesting. Appointed American envoy to Turkey in 1849, Marsh tours Egypt, Palestine, Central Europe, and Italy, taking note, often from atop a camel, of defunct cities, worn-out river valleys, and strange deserts where human and natural histories intertwine. The overload of new information sends him rushing—where else?—to the renowned libraries of antiquity. "Only because he could read so many languages and explore so many ancient texts at first hand," writes William Cronon, a professor at the University of Wisconsin, "was Marsh able to gather the widely scattered evidence for his argument that the ancient civilizations of the Mediterranean had brought about their own collapse by their abuse of the environment." The fall of Rome, it turns out, was an issue of resource depletion and improper land management—the myth of limitless plenty getting the best of an entire civilization.

Marsh thinks back to his childhood, to the axes, to the denuded ridges. The ambassador from Vermont's "great insight built a bridge between these two points of his own lived experience," Cronon claims. "In the degraded environments of the Mediterranean he saw a prophecy of America's possible future."

It's a light-bulb epiphany, an illumination of connections heretofore unseen, and over the subsequent years it will only grow brighter and brighter. When Marsh commences the work of composing *Man and Nature* in 1860, his eyes are still weak from the early battle with the encyclopedia, but his *vision* is sharp.

⁂

That vision—the vision that went on to inspire conservation reforms in India, Australia, South Africa, and Japan, not to mention everything from the creation of the US Forest Service to the contemporary environmental movement in the United States—has a home. At 550 acres, the Marsh-Billings-Rockefeller National Historic Park is considerably less grand than, say, the Grand Canyon, but the terrain is stunning in its own mossy, ferny, Green Mountain way. Paths and dirt lanes wind through stands of sugar maples, red pines, and hemlocks on the flanks of Mt. Tom, the clear-cuts that once wrecked the surrounding countryside now only visible in a hiker's imagination. Established in 1998, Vermont's sole national park is unique among the 401 units in the federal system because of its mission statement: to tell the story of conservation history and the evolving nature of land stewardship in America. Yosemite has its soaring granite domes, Yellowstone its howling wolves. Woodstock has its local boy and his big book.

On a recent visit to the Carriage Barn Visitor Center—a

warm, woody museum-library boasting a thousand titles, comfortable chairs, and an environmental history display that runs from Ralph Waldo Emerson through Earth Day and beyond—I was greeted by Joe Herrick, his white hair just visible beneath the classic flat-brimmed park ranger hat. "What are you doing out there, building an ark?" he asked. It had been raining for three days, all across Vermont, and showed no sign of stopping. I mentioned an exuberant gang of second graders I'd encountered in the parking lot, their colorful slickers and muck boots lending a welcome flare to the otherwise dim weather. "I think of them as bees, and those yellow buses are the hives," Herrick said. "Hundreds of groups buzz through every year."

The comment made me smile, and not only because of the affection in Herrick's voice. Here was an indication that the "grandfather of conservation" might not be quite as obscure as I had thought. Marsh's life was written across the room's walls, bound in books lining the shelves, framed in black-and-white photos. One photo showed Woodstock in 1869, all bony pastures and bare hills. Another photo showed Marsh working at a sprawling desk on a third edition of *Man and Nature*, papers spread willy-nilly, a marble statue of some armless lady peering over his shoulder. Quotes were collaged with the images—excerpts from letters Marsh had written to friends, lines from lectures he'd presented to colleagues. In this welcoming space, so snug and cozy, *Man and Nature* was not a dead tome but a living presence, its message of balance and interdependence speaking across the ages.

"This year marks the 150th anniversary of its publication," Herrick said. "We're throwing a party but haven't firmed up our official plans yet."

In some ways a lot has changed since 1864, both for better and for worse; in others, nothing much is all that different. People talk about mass extinctions, global warming, and greedy corporate polluters as if these are new terrors, new problems. But maybe they're better understood as symptoms of some deeper, older problem. Maybe the real problem is no different than the one a nineteenth-century polymath faced in his time, and the Romans faced in theirs, and the children who so quickly become adults will face fifty or a hundred years down the line: *Homo sapiens* have a tremendous power, a power to destroy and to heal. We must restrain ourselves, must act as friends and helpers of the natural whole. It isn't easy and never will be. Things run amok. In Marsh's words, "Man has a right to the use, not the abuse, of the products of nature."

I got out my wallet to pay the entrance fee, happy to contribute a few dollars to a deserving institution. Ranger Herrick shook his head. "No charge," he said. "You're free to walk or read. It's your park." He tipped the brim of his hat, releasing a few beads of water onto the floor.

Mt. Tom was calling, misty and enchanted, and I was eager to stroll the land that opened George Perkins Marsh's eyes and mind. Starting for the door, I flipped up my raincoat's hood. I assumed I'd meet the kids somewhere on the trail, downpour be damned.

Autumn Snows

I was seven when I first beheld—was blown away by, bowed down to—the migrating flocks of snow geese that annually rest and feed on the Dead Creek Wildlife Refuge in western Addison County. My parents, having taken me on a foliage hike up nearby Snake Mountain, decided that dropping by the refuge would nicely round out the day. They were right: the day was rounded, as were countless others, and years also. Welcoming the traveling snow geese with a hello that is nothing more than quiet observation, perhaps a nod of the head, has become a tradition for me, a ceremony marking another turn of the seasonal wheel that is also the wheel of my life.

This past autumn, in addition to weekly sunrise birding field trips to the Refuge, I began browsing the vast scientific literature on snow geese (they are a particularly well-studied avian species). I did so with the hope of broadening my appreciation by broadening my understanding, not that my appreciation needed much help.

Three thousand white birds pouring up from yellow corn in a single fluid mass. Sharp nasal cries climbing one over another, arguing for space in the huge, empty air. And the

stillness, the stillness in the land and in myself when the
flock sinks out of view and goes silent, like a dream vanishing in the moment of waking. "Birds can calm you...can
draw irritation right out of you," says Barry Lopez in his
essay "A Reflection on White Geese." They can indeed. I've
felt it. But I wanted even more.

So I kept reading, kept reading, and a few mornings I even
met with the Fish and Wildlife Department biologists who
manage the refuge and the broader Wildlife Management
Area it belongs to. We talked natural history, conservation,
hunting, and the role that humans play in the snow goose's
migratory journey. These informative, enjoyable conversa-
tions took place beneath skies streaked with birds: lines of
birds, pods of birds, countless *V*s of varying size and font.
At times we would go silent, watching, rotating slowly like
weathervanes to take it all in. At other times I'd be alone, or
with friends, seconds sliding into minutes, minutes into the
bottomless pool of my attention.

Sure enough, it happened, just as I'd hoped. Here was
the beauty alongside the chaos and the calm, and here was
the little nod of my head. And here, too, was the context, the
narrative that lends nuance and substance to a Dead Creek
visit. It's the narrative of a life that is not my own, but that
crosses my path every year when the leaves go orange and
the nights go cold.

⁂ ⁂ ⁂

The global population of snow geese, estimated at 5 or 6
million, is divided into three distinct regional populations:

think Californians, Midwesterners, and New Englanders, each group defined by its native slice of longitude. The sub-species seen in Vermont—the greater snow goose, *Chen caerulescens atlantica*—generally does not overlap with the other populations. It breeds on the summery tundra of Baffin Island, Ellesmere Island, and northwestern Greenland, as well as on the 1,600-square-kilometer southern plain of Bylot Island, in Nunavut Province. These sites are, roughly speaking, way the heck up above Quebec. Like the geese themselves, foreign place-names are a reminder that the world is always beyond what we know of it—always bigger, always more mysterious.

Scientists characterize the greater snow goose's migra-tion as "a combination of long stopovers with rapid and distant flights between areas." The first major stopover, on the Ungava Peninsula, east of Hudson Bay, lasts most of September. From there it's a sweeping view of the boreal forest, a landing executed with the grace of "waffling leaves" (Barry Lopez again), and a much-deserved meal of Ameri-can bulrushes on the Saint Lawrence River's upper estuary.

The *atlantica* population—which numbers around 1 million—moves in pulses, a flock of five hundred arriving on Tuesday, a flock of a thousand or more on Thursday. Looking close, one can see family units flying within the larger body of birds, the juveniles—usually three to five of them—distinguished from their parents by drabber plumage. Looking closer still, one might notice the rusty stains on the necks and faces of certain individuals; these are the veterans, old-timers that have grubbed about in the Saint Lawrence's iron-rich mud for many consecutive years. ("Grubbing" really is the scientific name for the snow goose's style of foraging on buried root masses, called rhizomes.) And as long as we're on the topic of elderly birds, I'll mention that the longest-lived snow goose on record was aged at twenty-six years and seven months, which, coincidentally, is just about my own age at the time of this writing.

By early October, the bulk of the population has settled on the Saint Lawrence estuary or on adjacent agricultural lands. This is known as "staging." I imagine a white-feathered raft miles long undulating in silky light; I imagine the raft coming apart, rising, sprawling toward Montreal, then up the Richelieu River to Lake Champlain and its skies. Snows (as they're nicknamed) are known to fly at astounding elevations, sometimes so high that an observer only *hears* them. I imagine massive flocks up there in the realm of everywhere-clouds, orienteering by some unfathomable mix of magnetism, memory, winds, geographical cues, and innate know-how. Somehow, they pull it off each year, and come mid-October my imagination goes back on the shelf in trade for binoculars. The "Snowstorm," to borrow a local hunter's favored phrase, has arrived.

Many geese fly straight through Vermont, over to the Hudson River Valley and on to permanent wintering grounds scattered along the Atlantic coast from New Jersey to South Carolina (the largest congregation is on Delaware Bay). Other flocks opt for one last stopover before continuing south a few weeks later; generally the snow geese have left the Champlain Valley for good by late November. I asked David Sausville, the chief biologist at the refuge, what factors determine the date of departure from stopover sites in Vermont, and his response was straightforward: as long as there's open water for roosting, and waste grain for feeding, the birds will hang tight.

Perhaps when some people hear the word "refuge" they think "pristine nonhuman nature." This would be a mistake. From afar—say, from the summit of Snake Mountain—the Dead Creek Wildlife Refuge resembles the rest of the countryside rolling out toward Lake Champlain. This is dairy land, a patchwork of cornfields and hayfields interspersed with impoundments and natural waterways. Only up close does one notice that it's actually something different, unique.

Hunters, photographers, and bird-nerds like myself are barred access from the refuge's four-hundred-acre interior (we do our viewing from the perimeter, often from the designated pavilion just off Route 17). Even the refuge scientists try to steer clear of the refuge itself, not wanting to disturb the birds. Farmers, on the other hand, can be seen driving tractors back and forth *within* the refuge, waves of white spilling out behind them in a kind of avian wake.

Waste grain—that's what Sausville said. It's a major player in the snow goose story. The Fish and Wildlife Department leases the refuge lands to farmers, but they do so with a few strings attached, strings that lead directly back to the bellies of the geese. At harvest time the farmers are required to leave a percentage of their crop standing, thus providing protective cover for the geese, and they aren't allowed to plow until after the first of November. This way, whatever grain doesn't make it into the combine is available on the surface of the fields for the geese to feed on. As it turns out, if it weren't for this gleaned banquet of leftovers, the geese would go elsewhere.

In fact, the Dead Creek snow geese *have* been going elsewhere, though it's unclear exactly where. "It's not unusual for goose populations to shift their migration routes if conditions warrant it," Sausville told me. The Snow's route, while fixed at a large scale (known as the North Atlantic Flyway), is flexible when it comes to specific stopover sites. I liken it to a sand dune, creeping this way and that through a sequence of years, but never leaving the beach. Sausville has a hunch that some of the geese that once frequented Addison County have moved to New York, where harvesting practices for grains (to supply poultry farms) are less efficient, resulting in more of the tasty waste. The birds follow the grub—it's that simple.

Snow geese didn't use the Dead Creek Refuge until the early 1980s, and even then they were a rare species in Vermont. Over the course of about fifteen years, though, the bird's presence on the refuge grew and grew, peaking at around twenty thousand individuals in 1998. These were the days of my childhood, of madness and bliss, birds blotting out the Adirondacks, clouding the ears and eyes and mind. Recent autumns have seen a high of around thirty-five hundred birds on the refuge, which, though a relatively low number, is still impressive, stirring, wonderful.

While Dead Creek is slowly (and only temporarily?) losing its birds, at the global scale the snow goose population is gaining exponentially. The explosion is directly attributable to the farmland grubbing that is now so central to this species' migration and wintering habits (more food equals increased reproductive success and increased survivorship). Remembering that in the early 1900s there were only a few thousand snow geese in the wild, today's ecologists worry about the geese eating themselves out of their sensitive Arctic house and home, triggering their own population collapse. All of this just goes to show that in nature nothing is constant. Everything moves, booming and busting. The presence of these birds in my life, and my valley, is not a guarantee, but a privilege.

⁂

In the essay I mentioned earlier, "A Reflection on White Geese," Barry Lopez describes the collective vocalization of a flock of Snows as "distant French horns and kettledrums," "rattled sheets of corrugated tin," "the cries of athletic young men at a distance," "a barking of high-voiced dogs, like terriers," "the squealing of shoats," "the cheering of a crowd in a vast stadium," "whoops and shouts," and "startled voices of outrage, of shock." Not to be outdone by his own free-ranging associations, he also musters an impressive array of visual images: "long skeins," "long scarves," "a wind," "a blizzard," "great swirling currents," "shoals of fish," "sliding walls." When a few thousand geese bank against a headwind, they are "feathers in the wing of a single bird."

Lopez's method is obvious—set a flock of metaphors loose across the blank sky of the page and maybe, just maybe, an impossibly surreal and moving spectacle will in some small way come to life inside the reader. I respect this approach. It embraces the fact that no one image, no one description, no one angle, is ever sufficient when it comes to contemplating, or experiencing, the natural world. Science. Literature. Emotion. Spirit. These are our tools. We must use and enjoy them all.

Three thousand white birds pouring up from yellow corn in a single fluid mass. Sharp nasal cries climbing one over another, arguing for space in the huge, empty air. And the stillness, the stillness in the land and in myself when the flock sinks out of view and goes silent, like a dream vanishing in the moment of waking.

Riding the Watershed

My first outing, on a muggy morning in early June, takes me south along Addison County's mostly straight, flat roads. I cross Little Otter Creek where it rushes and froths through a gorge beneath a bridge. I pass an osprey's bulky stick-nest set atop a telephone pole, twisting on my seat to glimpse wings lifting, the bird curving away through a cloud-mottled sky. The blacktop is smooth, then rough, then smooth, sometimes patterned by dirty tractor tires, sometimes clean. I weave through traffic in downtown Vergennes, traverse vast hayfields, sing howdies to chomping cows, wipe sweat from my eyes with the back of a hand. Green-and-white signs depicting a bicycle lead me on: more fields, a sleepy village, a red barn fading to gray. Somewhere nearby but out of sight, the valley's low wet heart beats and beats, easing ripples to shore.

Five days later—days of work and driving and computers and not enough outdoors—I'm on it again, this time up north. My pal Sean meets me at Oakledge Park in Burlington and off we go, chitchatting, swerving, joking. The bike path is crowded but pleasant, a slalom course of dogs and joggers and other riders, some on mountain bikes, some on road bikes, some on cruisers. Streets and brick buildings spill down the hill to the waterfront. Sailboats in the harbor rock on their moorings, their rigging tinkling. We poke along for an hour, inland through a neighborhood, through parts of Colchester I've never seen, then back out to the lake. Aluminum water. Extensive views. The path becomes the Causeway, an old raised railroad bed arcing across the mouth of the Inland Sea to dead-end at the Cut, a gap just shy of South Hero that allows boat passage to the Broadlake. From mid-June through Columbus Day a pontoon barge known as the "bike ferry" motors riders across the Cut for a nominal fee. Not Sean and I, not today. A light rain comes and goes, falling in screens, and we turn around.

Another week, another ride, another twenty, thirty, forty, or fifty miles. I'm more of a walker, really, more comfortable bushwhacking in boots than rolling on rims, but when summer rises out of mud season's slop and squishy weather, rises vibrant and inviting, I do find myself drawn to the Champlain Bikeway. The route is like a line of music, a melody played over and over again by different instruments. A swim, a maple creemee, a fox in a vegetable garden, a short steep hill, a quart of fresh-picked strawberries, a Revolutionary War fort, a paved road, a pothole road, a family of four riding straight at me, helmets shiny—the variations are endless, the textures always changing. As Heraclitus says: You can't put your foot in the same bikeway twice. Or something like that.

The 363-mile bikeway marks an oval around Lake Champlain and makes me think of the Ouroboros, the mythological snake that eats its own tail, symbol of eternal renewal. A journey commences in Shelburne, Vermont, or Crown Point, New York, or Sabrevois, Quebec, or Panton, Vermont, or Ausable, New York, or anywhere between. You can bike to Whitehall, where Wood Creek flows in from the south, or you can bike to Saint-Jean-sur-Richelieu, where the Richelieu River flows northward to the St. Lawrence. As with the snake, neither of these are true beginnings or endings. The lake eats its own tail, pulling water from the hills that pull water from the sky, returning it to the oceans and the air only to be filled with it again. Picture a wheel endlessly rotating. Water cycle. Bicycle. Lots of cycles here.

I haven't pedaled the entire bikeway; I haven't even come close. Thirty-five subloops, each with a name and character all its own, veer from the principal route to form a thousand-mile network. *Rebel's Retreat* sets working farms against an Adirondack backdrop. *A Trail to Two Beaches* inscribes a figure eight with a state park at either end. Some folks spend a single afternoon exploring, while others bike from B&B to B&B as part of an organized tour, a hired van shuttling clean clothes and toiletries to each night's destination. Ferries cross the lake at Shoreham, Charlotte, Burlington, and Grand Isle, lending even greater flexibility to route design.

A few years ago, having just concluded a cross-country drive, my good friend Ross stretched his legs with a multiday adventure on the bikeway. "I had time before I had to be back at work, and I was stiff from too many hours in the car," he tells me. "I threw some panniers on the bike, a sleeping bag, some food, printed out some maps from the website, and went for it." He pedaled north from home in Charlotte with a stiff tailwind at his back, unsure where he would sleep and not the least bit concerned. His goal was the full circuit. "As long as that wind was blowing, I was going,"

Vineyards, orchards, a marina, a father and son baiting their hooks—it was April, sunny without being hot. Ross worked his way onto the Champlain Islands, up the Alburgh Tongue, and across the border into southern Quebec's agricultural plains, land so blank it smacks of Saskatchewan. Bowing his head to the soothing monotony of the terrain, he lost himself for a time in the trance of endurance. Then, an hour before sunset, a local cyclist appeared, a French Canadian fellow with a house nearby. "He invited me to come over for dinner and crash in the guest bedroom for the night," Ross says. "I played soccer with his kid, slept well, and in the morning they fed me a sort of European-style breakfast: toast, thinly sliced ham, fresh fruit. It wasn't your typical American bowl of Wheaties, but it got me on my way."

Tagging the northernmost point on the bikeway early that second day, Ross made a U-turn, switched to the west side of the Richelieu, and found himself swept up in a rainstorm. There was nothing to do but ride. He cranked south along the New York shore for hours, the wind that had been his helper now cold and sharp in the face. "By the time I hit Plattsburgh I was one seriously drowned rat," he says. "I went into a laundromat and popped some coins in the dryer, stuffed in all the clothes I had, and sat there in my bike shorts and undershirt, feeling a little awkward." Back on the road, the rain increased, steadied, multiplied itself by five. A slice of pizza from a general store helped take the edge off, but it didn't last. "At Essex I could sense my warm cozy bed across the lake. I'd ridden over a hundred miles that day already, nearly all of it in a downpour." He hopped the ferry to Charlotte, calling it good, knowing that the bikeway would be there for him another time.

I think it's important to emphasize that when Ross undertook this mission he was fresh off a two-month solo road trip around the American West, a trip that had gobbled up more than a dozen states and innumerable ecosystems. He'd been away a long time, his senses steeped in desert sounds and coastal smells and alpine light, in the moods of places so different from the Champlain Basin. It wasn't just stiff legs and a craving for exercise that put him in the saddle as soon as he arrived home. Rather, it was a desire to reconnect, to engage. It was an urge to welcome himself back, physically, personally.

I can imagine living in a different time and a different culture, one where it would be unremarkable to speak of Lake Champlain as a god or deity. One hundred twenty miles long, 12 miles wide, 580 miles of crinkled coast—the lake is big, powerful to behold; it shapes the earth and the lives of those who dwell in its basin. Eighty-one fish species slip through dark depths and sun-shot shallows. Three hundred eighteen species of birds hunt liquid surfaces, roost on overhanging trees, nest in marshes, visit during migration. The Tibetan Buddhists make ritual circumambulations of holy mountains: Kailash, Lapchi, Kawa Karpo. To circumcycle Lake Champlain is to cross thirty-one major tributaries and dozens of smaller streams draining an 8,234-square-mile watershed. It's to become the ring on a 6.8-trillion-gallon bathtub holding drinking water for some two hundred thousand people. Whether riders on the bikeway think of it this way or not, to circumcycle the lake is to wrap oneself around the low wet center, to hug that softly beating heart.

Ross: "The lowlands by the lake are a different environment than the foothills. We think of Vermont as craggy, and it is for the most part, but the bikeway keeps things pretty smooth. It's a different perspective. Champlain seems like the edge, you know, the border, but then you start tracing it and you realize it's the middle, that everything is organized around it. The views of the mountains keep changing. You keep riding. You go farther and farther and it's hard to stop."

Another week, another outing, another bikeway. Here I am, alone, riding into haze and humidity, my ears full with the drone of insects in tall grass and the whir of tires against the road. What began as an easy meander has become a hunched, huffing grind—the pleasure of the pain of pushing hard. Fenceposts blur. An osprey cuts a cloud. The lake, ah, the lake is only a mile or two away; I can practically taste it, smell it, feel it around me. My bike leaned against a tree or laid on smooth blue stones at the water's edge, I'll swim a hundred strokes, another hundred, a hundred more. I don't wear spandex shorts when I ride—I wear a bathing suit.

Ratbird Overwhelm

I wanted to fill my mind with birds, with cormorants, and that meant first emptying my mind of thoughts. In my experience, there's no better way to cultivate this interior blankness than a ten-mile kayak, solo, up the middle of Lake Champlain. I put in south of Essex on a fine June morning, my usual coffee-brain buzzing its usual buzz, and within an hour the measured *dip-dip* of the paddle had lulled me into a pleasing stupor. Perfect. By the time I reached Four Brothers Islands, around noon, my consciousness rivaled the water's smoothness.

From afar the islands were nothing—a smudge on the horizon, a tan smear. Then, one stroke at a time, the picture came into focus: two flat slivers to the west, two cliffy plugs to the east. If I didn't know better, I would have said these were lifeless skerries, barren wastes. But I did know better. I kept paddling, kept scanning, and soon the day's vast blue was speckled, the specks swarming like hordes of mosquitoes, like the Brothers were the heads of giant earthen swimmers coming up to breathe. A few minutes later, a dark shape beating past the sun released a foul spray across the brim of my ball cap.

Did I just get…

Yes, friend, you did. Squarely so.

The Four Brothers microarchipelago, located one and a half miles from the tip of Willsboro Point, is Lake Champlain's humble answer to the breeding seabird colonies of the North Atlantic. Owned by the Adirondack Chapter of the Nature Conservancy, and closed to human foot traffic, it provides a seasonal home (one scientific report used the word "mecca") for approximately 24,000 ring-billed gulls, 250 herring gulls, 50 great blue herons, 300 black-crowned night herons, and 4,000 double-crested cormorants—essentially the entire Champlain Basin population of this last species.

"Chaos is order. Order is a mystery. Time is meaningless." That's how Franklin Russell described a similar spot in *The Secret Islands*, his book of avian explorations off the Newfoundland coast. "The deep-throated roar of the colony cries out to a heedless sky. The human observer, cowed by its primitive energy, by its suggestion of the unnamable, stumbles on blindly."

Approaching the first Brother, I wasn't stumbling, exactly, my legs crammed into the kayak's narrow bow, but my senses were tripping over themselves, sight and smell and sound and taste tangling in a synesthetic knot. Is that rotten funk on the tip of my tongue or in the burrow of my nose? Am I seeing or hearing these hundreds of fanning wings?

I glided in close to a stony beach where dozens of cormorants watched me with creepily mesmerizing jade-green eyes. The lake at my back was feathered—a quivering raft of birds—and then, so quick, the sky above was feathered, the entire beach launched into riotous flight. Better keep the expensive binoculars in their case, I thought, bombs exploding stem to stern, near misses splashing starboard and port. I jotted down a single word in my journal, and just as the pencil came away a shot landed on the page, splotching out the *over*, leaving only the *whelm*.

Overwhelm: to present with an excessive amount; to affect deeply in mind or emotion; to defeat completely and decisively.

Did I just get...

Yes, friend. Like we said: Welcome.

⁜ ⁜ ⁜

The night before this trip, chatting at a backyard barbecue, I mentioned my plan to a buddy's mother—how I would immerse myself in the presence of *Phalacrocorax auritus*; how through long hours of unbroken observation I would inch up to the edge of me and plunge into the depths of them; how, basically, it would be friggin' awesome. Her response, wrung like dishwater from a dramatically scrunched face, was immediate and emphatic: "But it stinks out there."

It certainly does, I replied. Stinks to high heaven, stinks like hell, stinks as only regurgitated bits of yellow perch, rainbow smelt, and alewife can stink, as only pounds upon pounds of gloppy, acidic, vegetation-killing feces can stink. It's real, I insisted. It's raw. Do you know the work of Franklin Russell? There are suggestions of the unnamable on these islands. Primitive energies!

The face scrunched tighter: "Cormorants are greasy. And gross. You're telling me you actually like them?"

To be clear, this was a professional horticulturist I was speaking with, a woman passionate about flowers and insects and countless other intricately evolved life-forms; a woman who only moments prior had noted with appreciation a cardinal singing from a nearby hedge. All God's creatures deserve a place in the choir, right? Wrong. Cormorants sing out of tune, as it were. She didn't say it explicitly, but it was obvious that she considered them pests, if not a plague. They were, literally and figuratively, on her shit list.

Having grown up on Lake Champlain, I knew the prosecution's case by heart. Exhibit A: ratbirds possess voracious appetites, consuming three times their weight each day, and are thus a potential threat to fisheries. Exhibit B: ratbirds compete with other colonial species over prime nesting habitat, displacing, for example, great blue herons and black-crowned night herons. Exhibit C: ratbirds destroy both the ecology and aesthetics of islands, whitewashing trees and shrubs, breaking off twigs to use in courtship displays, leaving places like the Four Brothers degraded and disgusting. Oh yeah, can't forget Exhibit D: they're ratbirds, ratty and ragged, a far cry from the elegant tern, the graceful egret, the enchanting loon, the majestic eagle.

But perhaps most damning is the matter of ascendance, the sheer numbers. Prior to 1981, no cormorants bred on Lake Champlain. By 1999 the population had grown geometrically to more than twenty thousand individuals. Noticeable newcomers, big and gangly and charcoal-colored, they mar the clean slate of How It Once Was and How It Ought to Be—which is to say they make for easy targets. I've even heard inebriated vigilantes brag of bowling for "rats" with Chris-Craft ski boats and 100-horsepower Evinrude motors.

Here's another way to articulate the tension: biological carrying capacity and social carrying capacity for cormorants do not always match; the local environment may give the go-ahead to flourish, but that doesn't mean anglers and shoreline homeowners will necessarily agree. It's a Goldilocks situation—too many, too few, ah, just right. One scientific study, "Attitude Strength and Social Acceptability of Cormorant Control Programs on Lake Champlain," found that the majority of New Yorkers and Vermonters surveyed supported current practices such as the hazing of nesting birds, egg oiling to prevent hatching, and state-sponsored shooting. "Population control techniques employed by wildlife management agencies rely on some degree of vilification of the cormorant," the authors wrote.

Vilification. Right.

My buddy's mother stared at me, her eyebrows arching while, somehow, the rest of her face remained scrunched. "Really? You're telling me you actually *like* them?"

⁂ ⁂ ⁂

According to the famous ecologist Aldo Leopold, the way of wild animals is to "suck hard, live fast, and die often." So true. Everywhere, all around me, cormorants were making Aldo proud, the hard-sucking cycle of life and death repeating itself, the biological wheel rolling up and over the height of yet another breeding season and on toward the next.

Cormorants in withered buckthorn thickets nested tenement-style, the ground below them a crowd of milling birds. Cormorants hardly two weeks old, their downy heads tipped back and swaying, mouths open to the possibility of a meal, made sounds like rusted screws ripped from a weathered deck. Cormorants in a single-file line swerved around a corner, fifty of them rising and banking as one fluid being, sinuous and silky, carving the invisible air almost into visibility.

They dove. They dripped. A cloud of gulls billowed up and was slashed apart instantly by a loner's quick black flight.

Throaty gurgle. Nasal squawk.

Splish-splosh!

Soaring shadows and shattered reflections.

What did Franklin Russell say? Time is meaningless? I'd completely lost track, the Overwhelm serving as a kind of warp or wormhole, a portal to some purely sensorial relationship with my surroundings that unfolded only in the present tense (yet felt like forever). The paddle was stowed across my lap, the journal tucked into my pocket, the binos safe in their poop-proof case. Drifting dazedly, I imagined myself as a floating island, a fifth Brother musing on the relentless comings and goings, the crazy commotion of the scene.

My kayak bumped into a beach—same beach as earlier? which Brother is this?—and I glanced up to see four adults in a nest balanced precariously on a sloping, splattered ledge. They were fighting, the fight a confusion of necks and wings, a mad writhing bouquet. A beak pinched a leg. Another beak clamped a third beak shut. One bird escaped only to turn right around and peck violently at whatever it could reach: a face, a webbed foot, the shifting spaces between bodies. Meanwhile, a mere three feet to the left, six more adults perched perfectly, sculpturally still, and two feet farther along four more adults struck poses. And behind them a pair of juveniles did some kind of raucous dance (or maybe they were gagging). And behind them there was a heron, a tern, a handful of swallows scooping and looping after each other.

Twisting in my seat to peer into the tinted shallows off my stern, I gasped; here was a face, the eye socket empty, the skull blanched, the entire image bending, ripples on the surface distorting it like a funhouse mirror. I wanted to look elsewhere but I was hypnotized, helpless. In the Overwhelm there's no such thing as stopping for lunch, and now my blood sugar was failing me, the visions coming sharper and weirder. That heron resembled a wizard in a flowing cloak, didn't he? That tern was wearing red lipstick, right? This pale wobbling skull was... grinning. Birds can grin?

For a fleeting but vivid moment I perceived the entire archipelago as a human maternity ward, thousands of wailing babies and their exhausted mothers packed in tight. Then it was a morgue, then a buffet, then a rock concert. Then it was nothing but primitive energy, a suggestion of the unnamable, the Adirondack skyline rising bluish in the background.

"Really? You're telling me you actually *like* them?"

The question emerged from the ornithological din as classical music sometimes emerges from the white noise of a waterfall; or perhaps I was just remembering. Either way, I responded as best I could: No, I said, silently and passionately. No, it's not that I *like* them. It's that I'm *amazed* by them, by the simple biological *fact* of them, by the sheer exuberant gnarly out-of-control *drive* of them, that's all. Maybe they should be culled to maintain some balance. Fine. But recognize that they are here and we are here and that being here together presents us with an opportunity. Recognize that beneath our data and management concerns and arguments and attitudes and reactions at backyard barbecues— beneath our thinking and feeling—there exists a miracle. Some call it Life, others Creation. In British coastal towns you can find statues honoring cormorants. On Erhai Lake in China, the species is revered. Sure, they stink—stink to high heaven, stink like hell—but if we paddle long enough and pay close enough attention and do the work of opening ourselves to that stink's awful...

I was cut off mid-rant by a silvery rain in my periphery, a shimmering veil sweeping in my direction, a gossamer mirage that was not a mirage and was not in my periphery— that was instantly all over the brim of my hat.

Again? I grabbed my paddle and pushed away, yearning for open water and birdless skies.

Adirondacks Inside Out

The sun is shining, warming a shallow pool we call the Bathtub. I'm a few years old, sitting there in my bathing suit, dabbling, the main body of Lake Champlain only feet away. To the west, beyond the water's flatness, a wall of mountains rises into sky—Whiteface, Hurricane, Marcy, so many fuzzy ridges, none of which I know by name, all of which I will remember.

So begins my relationship with the Adirondacks.

What does it mean that this range, this region, filled my eyes and mind at such a young age? What does it mean that this view and a thousand variations on it—from the car, from the local sledding hill, from the bedroom window— formed the backdrop of my youth and growing up? What does it mean that these particular shapes and colors, *Adirondack* shapes and *Adirondack* colors, accompanied me through so many days and months, so many seasons and weathers, so many changes of light and changes of myself?

It's February and I'm a boy skating on frozen bays, Giant Mountain's east-facing slabs winking with bright snow. It's June and I'm a teenager sneaking beers at sunset, drinking them in a kayak, feeling an ecstatic buzz as I drift and wobble and gaze deeper than I'd thought possible into the layered, folded distance. It's early spring, cold and blustery, and I'm an adult. I'm standing by the Bathtub, high cumulus clouds inking the far foothills with their traveling shadows. I've climbed a couple dozen of the forty-six major peaks in the range, camped for weeks in the muddy woods, portaged crooked trails often enough to fear my neck might never straighten from the weight. Been there—paddled, groveled, slapped mosquitoes, built fires—done that. And now I'm here again, hood up, squinting and remembering, wondering how everything hangs together.

A Vermonter, born and raised, that's me. When I look across the lake I sense a green heart, a secret pulsing interior, and I recognize that there is so much I don't know and won't ever know about the Adirondacks. Landscape photography has been criticized for flattening its subject, for reducing the three-dimensional earth to a screen, a poster, a two-dimensional imposter. What's it like to know those ridges and valleys across the water—their textures and moods, their hums and clicks and tints and shades and subtleties—from the *inside*, as a native? A photo has no answers, and you could argue that what I have of the Adirondacks, despite my visits, despite my efforts, is one long photo, the camera's shutter left open for three decades.

An outsider with an outsider's view, that's me. Yet I can't help but also think of myself as something bigger, something broader, my identity more expansive. I struggle to hold two truths at once, both of which can be found on the same page of an essay by Gary Snyder. One: "Landscapes have their own shapes and structures, centers and edges, which must be respected." Two: "These boundaries are not hard and clear, though. They are porous, permeable, arguable."

Do the Adirondacks permeate Vermont? Does Vermont permeate the Adirondacks? Am I porous, soaked with both?

⁕ ⁕ ⁕

In his book *Wandering Home*, Bill McKibben, a one-time Adirondack resident who resides these days in the Green Mountains, writes: "To me, this country on either side of Lake Champlain, though it has no name and appears on no map as a single unit, constitutes one of the world's few great regions, a place more complete, and more full of future promise, than any other spot in the American atlas." What interests me is not the glowing praise but that notion of "a single unit." McKibben is thinking bioregionally. He's thinking of the Champlain Basin as a watershed, of the lake as a center rather than an edge.

Once, years ago, rowing a wooden boat on a gilded evening, my oars spread wide like wings, I *had* it—the feeling of all those streams gathering there beneath me at the low middle, east and west drawn together, unified in a shared search for the sea. But such moments are fleeting, an awareness like water in the hand. A page after mentioning the "single unit," McKibben goes on to note that, for most people, most of the time, Lake Champlain divides the land "neatly into two very different kingdoms of the imagination." I don't like it, but I think he's right.

Again and again I've tried to stitch the two different kingdoms together into a single fabric. For a needle I've used my own body, for thread my own zigzag paths. One summer I worked at a camp in Vermont, leading teenagers on wilderness trips in the High Peaks. Another summer I painted a friend's cottage on Rainbow Lake, fishing each evening in cool wind when the day's labor was finished. And then there was the exhausting experiment that some buddies and I undertook, an experiment that involved loading bicycles into a canoe at dawn, paddling across the lake to Split Rock Point in Essex, riding from there through Elizabethtown to the trailhead for Hurricane Mountain, climbing the mountain, napping up top, and finally retracing our route back to Vermont, arriving home as the blushing sun fell away for the night.

As I say, these have been efforts, conscious attempts to reconcile two visions, two perspectives, two experiences— the Inside and the Out. I stand on my porch, a mug of tea steaming in hand, and trace the horizon that the day before or the season before or the decade before I traced with my own body. I stand on the summit of Vermont and look west. I stand on the summit of New York and look east. Between these prominences, down in the basin where the lake shines silver, I see my life going about its business.

And always, always I end up back at the Bathtub.

So here I am, a cold and blustery morning, the waves like galloping horses with frothy manes. It's early spring and the lake is high with runoff, with melted snow that no longer goes by "Adirondack" or any other name. I've been reading a book of essays by David Hinton, a translator of ancient Chinese poetry, and there's this line I can't get out of my head: "Things are themselves only as they are part of something else."

Whiteface faces me with its white face. Hurricane nuzzles the atmosphere. Marcy reposes in the south. The Bathtub is underwater but somehow I'm still a dabbling child. Looking as I always have. Looking as I always will.

The Great Derangement

My relationship with the Great Range Traverse has from the beginning been characterized by suffering. Not just any type of suffering, but a unique brand of Adirondack mind-body-soul suffering that hints at depths, mysteries, possibilities. Twenty-five miles long, nine peaks, damn near eighteen thousand feet of up and down, up and down, up and down—the GRT isn't just some hike. The trail is black mud, balance-beam logs, ladders, ledges, loose footing, exposed slabs, and more than the occasional awkward scrambling maneuver. It's a summer's worth of hiking packed into a single hike, a summer's worth of knee pain and lung burn condensed into a single drawn-out wince.

I first heard of the GRT from a magazine article that ranked it the third-hardest day hike in the country, referring to the chain of mountains whose heights it traces as a "murderers' row." My friends and I were eager, energized, ready-for-adventure sixteen-year-olds at the time, all for being murdered. But twenty-five miles in a day? We drove to the Rooster Comb trailhead, in Keene Valley, planning to tick off the initial eight peaks on Saturday, camp at Panther Gorge that night, and climb 5,344-foot Marcy—the last murderer in the lineup—on Sunday morning before hiking out.

Rooster Comb, Lower Wolfjaw, Upper Wolfjaw, Armstrong, Gothics, Saddleback, Basin, Haystack: read these not as ink marks on the page but as waves rising one after another, each cresting higher than the last; better yet, read them as the mountains they are, those spaces between the names so many sharp notches and cols. By the time we reached Panther Gorge at sundown we were dead on our blistered, aching, mashed-up feet. Murdered indeed. We laid a tarp on the ground and passed out, only to be rousted by the dawn what seemed like ten minutes later.

I remember nothing of the climb up Marcy that morning, nor do I remember how we managed to miss the turnoff for the so-called easy part of the GRT, the nine-mile, mostly rolling trail that would have led us through the Johns Brook Valley and back to the parking lot's blessedly flat ground. What I do remember is feeling so desperate to get off the ridge that, come afternoon, we decided to attempt a shortcut via the other side of the range. Sweat-soaked, half-dumb with fatigue, crumpling inward on ourselves, we incorrectly figured that nothing could be worse than more of the same.

You're probably familiar with bushwhacking, but lakewhacking? Yeah, neither were we. And then, just like that, our packs were balanced atop our heads, the dark waters of Lower Ausable Lake creeping up our necks as the mucky floor sank away. One friend fell and cut his shin against a rock. Blood went everywhere. In lieu of a first-aid kit, we did our best to bandage the wound with a wool sock before continuing on.

And on. And on and on. Miles lengthened. Time slowed. It felt as though I'd passed through some invisible barrier, broken into an altered world. Derangement: "a state of mental disturbance and disorientation." The trees and stones were the same but different; the sock became a red thing—crusty, dusty, not a sock at all. That evening, when we found the car, the range behind us wasn't the range we'd climbed into the day before, and we were something else, too, though *what* exactly is hard to say.

⁙ ⁙ ⁙

Which leads me to my most recent GRT outing, an everything-at-once-grit-and-tenacity-knock-it-off-in-a-single-day experiment in exhaustion-consciousness. The idea was simple: if the GRT is going to kick your ass and twist your brain, why not embrace the suffering as a means of cultivating some unique perspective on the natural world? Why not become a doe sprinting though the underbrush, branches snapping, cobbles rolling under hoof, a mountain lion hot on your juicy white tail? What would the Great Range look like through *her* blurry, bloodshot eyes?

We started hiking with sunup on one of those July days that's so long it begins around midnight—a stump-tough pal who'd proved his stump-toughness on the original bloody sock escapade, another friend who is best described as stoical and goatish, and me. The pink sky was brightening toward blue, the birds singing loud enough to hurt. When we made a wrong turn, adding an extra mile to the hike, our response was laughter, ebullience. What's another 5,280 feet when you've still got 126,720 to go?

Romping over braided roots and lichened stones, the damp, mossy, intricate woods enveloping us, I told my friends about a guy I'd gone to college with who jogged twenty-five to thirty miles a day, every day, exclusively on mountain trails; he was after a certain type of bliss, this guy, a moment where he and the environment became one, where he achieved a point of personal brokenness that rendered him totally open, totally fluid.

"Whoa," the Goat and Stump said in near-perfect synchronization.

"Yeah," I said. "And did I mention that he often runs barefoot?"

More conversation. A brisk trot across the Wolfjaws. From Armstrong a view of things to come: big wild slopes, gleaming off-white slide paths, countless secret nooks where a hermit-sage might set up shop, sip tea, and contemplate for decades the earthly grandeur. We rushed without being in a rush, stopping now and then for a salamander or dewy spiderweb. Then, as anticipated, the pep in our legs escaped, taking with it our delight in details. If the spiderwebs were still there, we charged through them unknowingly. Mouths open. Sucking air and gossamer.

Forget what I said earlier. Gothics, Saddleback, Basin, these aren't waves or mountains; they're cramps, scraped knuckles, disconcerting twinges in the hamstrings. When we reached the summit of bald, beefy Haystack, thirteen-some-odd miles deep, all three of us were in the déjà vu of peak after peak after peak. A quick glance into the depths of Panther Gorge made the decision easy: it was time for lunch. Salami, chocolate bars, hummus sandwiches, cookies, sliced turkey, fruit, brownies, cheddar cheese, mixed nuts—the meal was another mountain to climb. Thirty minutes later, doubly spent, I tried to stand. Nope.

"My dad's got an expression for this feeling," the Stump said with a smile, lounging like some Roman emperor garbed in quick-dry outdoor apparel, crumbs and whatnot in his beard. "Shot at and missed, shat at and hit."

It became our motto: shat at and hit! With considerable effort, though, I *was* able to get on my feet and I *was* able to pick steps down the ratty, eroded, dizzyingly steep trail and I *was* able to drag myself back up the other side of the gorge to the top of Marcy, apex of New York. That final climb pained me badly, but not in the hoped-for manner. Where was my weirdo-vision, my special view of nature, my hard-earned brokenness and transcendent communion? The thought crossed my mind that maybe I was stronger than I'd been in the past, that maybe I needed to push a little more forcefully these days to break through that invisible wall.

And then the more obvious thought came to me: you, sir, are a fool. Invisible wall? I'd gotten carried away. A long hike is just a long hike, not a gateway to an altered state of being or an enriched sense of place. Load it with all the fancy ecophilosophical ruminations you like, the GRT remains the GRT.

⁂

We took catnaps on Marcy's summit, wispy clouds moving across us like cooling blankets. No dreams. No revelations. As we descended into the Johns Brook Valley, a light shower fell across rays of sun, and for a moment I felt wholly renewed and happy, grateful for a sweet day in the hills, deranged or not. The shower passed, but the gratitude stuck with me as we meandered in a daze through the late afternoon hours and the immense, rain-freshened forest. The brook was in my ears, the drumming rhythm of my steps centered in awareness. We spread out along the trail, each man receding into his own private and not entirely unpleasant inner world—the Goat out front, the Stump second, and me, the weakest of the three, in the back.

Then farther back. Then even farther back. Then far enough back as to be totally alone in the graying, dimming dusk. We'd been on the move for fifteen hours and darkness was on its way. I still felt fine, though, didn't I? Yes, I said to myself, you still feel fine. But with less than a mile left it became officially undeniable: I didn't feel fine. I didn't feel even remotely *close* to fine. The rolling easy exit, as I should have known, was doing me in and doing me in good.

Hunched over with a knotted gut, hands on my hips, I staggered a curlicue, that awful metallic preheave tang on the back of my tongue. It was like my body knew the grueling workday was almost finished and had decided to cut out early, head to the bar for a couple of rounds with his friends. No, it was more vivid than that. It was like all the earth I'd touched since dawn—the toadstooly logs and stale puddles, the birch bark and pine needles, the buggy dirt and up-thrust chunks of rock—like it all had been sucked through my feet and legs and was now mixing in my belly alongside that smorgasbord lunch.

Was it really happening? Was I about to be thrown cranium-first through the invisible wall—the wall that I once again wholeheartedly believed to exist—by my churning stomach?

You won't believe me when I say it, but I tell you honestly, with the High Peaks as my witness, that I was no more than three-tenths of a mile from the parking lot when at last I couldn't take it anymore and lowered myself to the ground. Crawled on the ground. Collapsed on the ground. My legs in the trail, my face mere inches from a mat of brown moldering leaves, I was—to put a dirty thing cleanly—hit on the bull's-eye.

Whether it was derangement or not, whether the skeletal veins on those brown leaves glowed and sparked as they never had before, whether I was in fact seeing *through* those leaves to their hidden depths, their mysteries, their possibilities, well, that's hard to say. Just know that I lay there for a long while, murdered once again by the Great Range and its famous traverse—murdered by some unyielding and ancient truth of the land.

And this too: that on the interminably long drive home, between spells of contorted unconsciousness, we pulled over three times so I could stumble out into the roadside weeds and let the GRT roar through me.

Steep and Difficult of Ascent

The Trap Dike on Mt. Colden, partially climbed in 1837 by the geologist Ebenezer Emmons, is perhaps the oldest mountaineering route in North America. Picture a narrow canyon from the desert Southwest with eighty-foot walls. Now tilt it up so that it's carved into the side of a mountain. Run a waterfall down it. Paint it a gloomy gray. Mottle it with mosses. Fill it with loose rocks and countless slanting ledges. Emmons, an adventurous fellow, couldn't pass up the invitation. He deemed the route "steep and difficult of ascent."

In 1849 two nephews of David Henderson, cofounder of McIntyre Ironworks in the nearby village of Tahawus, climbed the dike, exited onto the slabs out right, and proceeded to Colden's 4,715-foot summit. An eagle flew overhead as if in mockery of this "first ascent." Though they were only out for a night, the cousins packed along bread, pork, tea, teapot, cups, blanket, compass, spyglass, ax, rifle, and a bottle of brandy nicknamed the "Admiral." They descended to Avalanche Lake, at the bottom of the route, where they'd stashed the gear prior to the climb. That afternoon they shot a deer for dinner. The next morning they caught trout for breakfast. More than 160 years later, though their style has yet to be duplicated, the route they pioneered remains *the* classic Adirondack scramble.

I first climbed the Trap Dike six years ago in January with my friend Craig. That was a miserable day—too cold to be warm, too warm to be dry. About a third of the way into the dike you encounter the route's crux, what British mountaineers call a "bad step." It's a nearly vertical pitch, maybe thirty feet high. The frozen waterfall we'd hoped to climb was rotten and soft—dangerous mush—so we roped up and climbed the neighboring rock with bare red hands and crampons on our feet. Many parties don't use a rope on the Trap Dike, but if they do, the bad step is where it comes out of the pack. We pulled over the lip, entered the upper dike, stowed the rope, continued another fifteen minutes through easier territory, then worked our way out onto the windy, crusty slabs. The slabs, though not that steep, are massively exposed. With a thousand-foot drop at our heels we kicked steps and plunged ice axes in fading light. The sun was setting when we gained the summit and started for the car via the standard ridgeline trail.

Craig and I returned to the Trap Dike last year. Neither of us had been back since our initial winter climb, and in the interim the route had undergone some changes, or so we'd heard. When Tropical Storm Irene raged through the Northeast in the autumn of 2011, it triggered a landslide high on Mt. Colden's west face. I searched some aerial photos on the Internet, and sure enough, the dike had received a scouring. Stunted spruce trees, mats of soil, pebbles and boulders—who knows how many pounds of debris were funneled into the dike and spit out the bottom. The photos showed a fan of rubble and splintered branches where a wooded slope once led from the lake up into the mouth of the dike. We wondered how the route had changed. Would it still be a classic? Would our hands and feet recognize it? Would Ebenezer Emmons?

. . .

The Saturday of the hike brought rain. We moved fast to stay warm, charging through deep mud, passing other folks on the trail: ten bedraggled kids with an adult chaperone in tow, a trio of middle-aged men wearing garbage-bag ponchos, French Canadian women smelling of shampoo. The sky was a thick, low cloud tangling the forest canopy.

Thanks to a thermos of coffee we weren't just hiking fast but also *talking* fast, mostly about Tom Patey, a Scottish climber who died before we were born. Patey stands out in the annals of mountaineering history as a particularly fervent champion of sloppy routes and sloppy conditions; he climbed in crap weather on crap rock, often pulling tussocks of alpine grass or clods of crumbling dirt should they appear at just the right moment. His was the art of Going For It, of Idiocy and Indefatigability. We agreed that he would have loved the Trap Dike in the rain.

After an hour-plus we reached Avalanche Lake. Cliffs rose from black water and disappeared in tattered, moving mist. A dead tree angled out from shoreline muck. We continued around the lake via slippery ladders and catwalks, eager to get a view across, up into the dike. Given the heavy weather, we could only see the rubble-fan and the lowest part of the route, below the bad step. Craig, who studied geology in college, speculated that given enough years, as more and more debris cascaded through the chute-like dike, it would fill the lake to form a bridge. Obviously, this would take millennia. In the meantime, we had to walk around.

At the south end of the lake a faint path veers left from the main trail, and a dozen steps later it frays out in a thicket. Craig said he'd take one for the team and pressed in at speed, the sopping shrubs brushing him down from below and above and both sides. Emerging onto the open rubble-fan five minutes later, we both looked and felt as if we'd been swimming. The deep, dark dike loomed above, its waterfall a zigzagging thread, sharp and white. *That's* our route? I pictured Patey in his grave, jealous.

Craig and I have been partners in mountain sketchiness for many years—in Colorado and California, in Scotland, all through the Adirondacks—and I've noticed a nervous pause, a sort of quiet fidgeting, that recurs at the base of each climb. I wandered off and peed, came back, adjusted my bootlaces, tucked in my shirt, adjusted my bootlaces again, checked that my shirt was tucked. Craig tightened his own laces and ate an apple, leaning against a rock. Already I felt myself growing chilled. We shrugged at each other, cinched our packs, and headed up through a series of broken ramps, the definition of scrappy terrain.

❖ ❖ ❖

Time contracts when the mind and body unite in focus, so I mean this quite literally when I say that we were standing in whirling spray at the foot of the bad step in no time flat. The waterfall was dumping and jumping, braiding and unbraiding, flying out and crash-landing. We'd lugged a short rope but didn't mention it; this was no place to mess with knots or talk. I stepped forward and about fifty garden hoses' worth of water caught my left knee. Moving right, balancing just outside of the main flow's gush, I left myself—or, even better, my self left *me*. Everything disappeared but the imperative: do not fall. I didn't *see* the edges and cracks in front of my nose so much as *feel* them. They felt cold and slick and solid.

It turned out that Irene's scouring was no match for the resilient dike. The old holds were there, and they led me, just as I remembered they would, to the bad step's baddest step, a psychologically intimidating final move where the waterfall runs between your legs as you stretch toward the relative safety of lower-angled terrain. I faced that move the only way I could—with horror, fascination, a touch of perverse joy, and not a modicum of grace—then stood off to the side snapping photos as Craig followed. Buzzed with adrenaline, we scampered and laughed our way through the upper dike to the exit onto the slabs. It was surreal out there, visibility maybe 150 feet, maybe less. My raincoat hood framed a long blur of dimples and fissures, green-yellow lichens, trickle-patterns. A bird cheeped from out of sight. The buzz faded and endurance took over.

On the summit we changed into dry shirts and winter

hats. Sitting on our packs, the clouds swirled close, making it feel as though we were in a snug room with billowing walls and, simultaneously, a dimensionless void, fluid and infinite. I'd forgotten my lunch but Craig had biscuits and bacon and a chunk of horseradish cheddar. We agreed that a nip from a bottle of brandy, "Admiral" or otherwise, would've hit the spot. For a half hour we snacked and talked: about peaks we'd climbed, about our long friendship in the mountains, about the face of the land, how it's always changing, always shifting and morphing, yet somehow always staying true to itself, always retaining its original identity. As the writer Edward Hoagland says of the natural world: "Flux itself is balance of a kind."

Staring into the overcast, our teeth beginning to chatter, we decided that the Trap Dike really is a classic. It's durable, a scramble for the ages. Then we went silent, no need to state the obvious—that it is, and will long be, steep and difficult of ascent.

Sledpacking

Let's make it clear: I was raised on the eastern shore of Lake Champlain, directly across from Essex, New York, and the Adirondack's High Peaks. I'm a Vermonter, yes, but I'm a Vermonter of the Champlain Basin, that wide lowland depressed thousands of years ago by glaciers unconcerned with modern political boundaries. I believe "home" is more than state, town, or household; it's the landscape of personal significance. My sun has always sunk behind the Adirondack skyline, my storms burst from its notches and gaps. Dix, Giant, Big Crow, Jay—these mark the rim of my home, the boundary separating what is known from what is waiting to be discovered.

At the age of nineteen, during a phenomenal year spent exploring the space between high school and college, two friends and I packed a car and drove over the Champlain Bridge and the fifty or so ice-fishing shanties dotting the frozen lake below. Having sledded many of the Green Mountain's premier hiking trails, I was interested in seeing what the Adirondacks might provide. Where better to begin than 5,344-foot Mt. Marcy, the state's highest peak? My friends, primarily interested in winter camping, left their sleds in the garage.

That's right, sleds—and I'm not talking Yamaha snow-mobiles. I'm talking that simple, classic toy so many children of the Northeast come to cherish long before setting foot on skis or snowboard. My sledding started with a straw-colored toboggan, a tiny neon snowsuit, and a family outing. From there, if you'll excuse the pun, it just snowballed.

By high school my buddies and I were sledding adult-sized mountains, the old summer hiking trails providing powdery troughs for our crazed races. Or maybe that should be *lunatic* races? One night we climbed a closed ski resort beneath a rising orange moon and rode groomed corduroy so fast it burned holes in our gloves. I frequented the local hardware store, replacing one busted sled after another, and spent evenings scrutinizing topographic maps, searching the contour lines for that Holy Backcountry Grail: the endless run.

Sledding didn't take itself seriously. It was goofy, floppy, rich in wipeouts. The carpenter's adage comes to mind: "Use the right tool for the right job." Sleds were the wrong tool for a mountain ridge, and in their wrongness they kept alive a winter pleasure that could so easily have slipped into memory and nostalgia. In the big forests on the big slopes, sledding whupped my butt and made me laugh like the child I once was—like the child I could, perhaps, forever be.

⁛ ⁛ ⁛

Wearing snowshoes and heavy packs—and in my case a ten-dollar plastic sled lashed to the latter with baling twine—my pals and I set off from the Adirondack Loj, in the direction of Mt. Marcy, also known as Tahawus, "The Cloud Splitter." Its rime-frosted dome had stood out on my personal horizon for years, always promising the butt-whupping of all butt-whuppings. Soon enough we would find out.

We slogged a handful of miles through rolling terrain, past lean-tos pillowed with snow. Late in the afternoon, our hips and shoulders sore beneath pack straps, we emerged from a narrow ravine onto the ice of Avalanche Lake. Algonquin's cliffs rose to our right. Mt. Colden's slabs glistened thousands of feet above us to the left. The lake shot out ahead, hoary and broad.

Winter travelers, whether polar explorers or Adirondack hikers, have been pulling their gear in sleds for years; which is to say that when I dropped my pack, rigged a towline out of the baling twine, and took a few steps to see how the loaded sled would glide, it was hardly a revolution. There is a photograph from that moment, though, a snapshot my friend took that captures the abundant cheerfulness of my personal discovery: sleds aren't just for bodies...packs can ride too! In the photo I'm smiling, doing a silly dance, about to blaze off across the lake with my loaded sled following like an obedient dog.

An hour before dark we made camp where Marcy's lower slopes ease into Lake Colden: built a fire, drank whiskey, ate bacon, hit the sleeping bags. The next morning we woke early and took turns breaking trail to the gusty, sunny, above-the-world-yet-entirely-of-the-world summit. I noted features as we climbed—ledges, banks of powder, a log with a mean-spiky branch. Barreling the steep trail at warp speed it would be hard to react to these obstacles. By necessity, the mental map grew with each observation, each labored step.

Up top, a hundred unsledded mountains circled us, beyond which Vermont's familiar peaks appeared rounded and blue in the distance. We ate snacks for a while, snugged up against a boulder, out of the wind. At last, I wrestled the sled to the snow and took a seat, securing my backpack in my lap before making final, nervous adjustments to balaclava and goggles. The trail extended from my toes in a straight line, plummeting over the summit's edge into a valley of sky.

Four miles and 2,600 feet back to camp. Should I have brought a helmet? Gravity's eternal mantra rang in my ears—*down, down, down.*

⁂

I'd like to say that I left my two buddies in a wake of glitter and exuberant laughter, never once stopping to scrape away the tears of triumph freezing my cheeks. I'd like to say that I was swept into a state of pure, egoless focus, my identity displaced as body and mountain fused though the sled's thin, brittle plastic. I'd like to say that my first descent of Mt. Marcy was the beefiest, burliest, most transcendent winter adrenaline rush of my life, the perfect culmination of years sledding and exploring the backcountry. I'd like to say it was the Grail, the run that goes and goes and keeps on going.

It wasn't. The descent was broken and jolted, too steep in some places, flat and bogged with snow in others; a few turns were so tight they shot me from the trail into a trap of gnarled dwarf firs. But it doesn't matter that the ride wasn't the pinnacle of air-catching, alpine elation. The hike, the haul, the camping, the whiskey and bacon, the enlivening wind and home-expanding views—these pushed the trip beyond a mere quest for adrenaline, pushed it into a kind of wholeness.

When I coasted into camp that evening I sat in my sled, chest heaving, friends ten minutes behind. A chickadee buzzed nearby, then flitted away, leading my eyes up to alpenglow ridges and the night's first stars. For a short while I was alone, wrapped in winter's stillness. I turned to look at the thin trail I'd cut through the snow and saw there the sled runs of my life laid out in sequence.

From a toddler's perspective a snowbank can be a mountain, but as we mature, the dinky hills of our early years lose their wild allure. In this I sense a fundamental theme: the aging human, the shrinking world, the incremental loss of frisky, playful youth. Sitting there, pulse slowing, sweat cooling, I knew for certain that sledding could be an adult vocation, a child's game grown up with the child—rugged, silly, committing, free. This is no longer sledding, I thought, more stars emerging from the growing dark, my pals' voices faint but increasing. This is *sledpacking*, and this is good.

That night we built another fire, swigged the remaining whiskey, finished the bacon. A warm dawn brought drizzling sleet and a scudding, bump-your-head sky that erased the mountain's tops. We struck camp and began the march back to the car, across softening Avalanche Lake, down into the dripping forest.

I dragged my sled most of the way that melty morning, happy enough to be hiking in the direction of dry socks and a crackling stove. At the crown of one small slope, though, I couldn't help myself; I prepped the sled and sat. The trail was slushy, I could barely keep my momentum, and I may or may not have toppled into a running creek—but that's all beside the point.

Frostbiting with Frostbiters

The trees are wind-flexed and the thermometer reads 4 degrees above zero. I dress in layers—thermal underwear, fleece tops and bottoms, two pairs of wool socks. Skiing? Snowshoeing? Nah. Been there, done that.

At the Ferrisburgh Town Beach, in the back of Kingsland Bay, half the gang's already waiting in the parking lot: Cathy Foley in red dry suit and yellow helmet; Tom Lamson in black dry suit, black tuilik, and black sunglasses; David Miskell, also in black, his white beard, red cheeks, and jolly guffaws reminding me of Santa Claus. A tuilik is a hooded jacket that flares out at the waist into a spray skirt. "These are neoprene," David says, "but in Greenland, where they were invented, they're made of sealskin. You'd be surprised how warm they keep you on a day like this."

David is a sixty-four-year-old organic farmer. He's also the founder and chief organizer of a group of winter kayak enthusiasts known as the Frostbiters. A couple years ago—"a good year"—he managed to get out on Lake Champlain at least once a week between November and March. That's what Frostbiters do: they get out. They get out into snowstorms, wide bays, smooth water, crying gulls.

They get out into numb appendages and extreme serenity. And miniature icebergs—can't forget those.

As a child I heard a news report about two fishermen lost in the middle of the lake when the ice broke loose around their shanty. In my youthful exuberance for all things adventurous and wintry, an exuberance I've yet to outgrow, it never dawned on me that their impromptu voyage might have been uncomfortable, unwanted, or, for that matter, anything short of awesome.

I phoned David a few weeks before Christmas, saying I'd like to accompany him on the water. "We do an annual New Year's Day paddle," he replied. "I'll try and round up some gear for you."

⁝ ⁝ ⁝

That gear is now overflowing the back of a Volvo station wagon, and David, who in his tuilik looks less like a traditional Santa than a scuba-diving Santa, is saying, "Okay, first let's get you into this dry suit." The suit resembles a kid's one-piece pajama jumper with footsies, tight rubber gaskets sealing the wrists and neck. After struggling for a few minutes, I'm zipped in snug. Neoprene booties, two neoprene fleece-lined hats, a pair of neoprene mittens, a PFD, and a spray skirt round out the outfit. I feel equal parts clunky and prepared.

Other folks show up—Wylie Rahill dressed in tan, Don Perley dressed in red—and that makes six of us. Our plan is to head south along the Vermont shore, then cross from Basin Harbor to the Palisades, a two-hundred-foot-tall band of cliffs rising sheer from the New York coast. It's a trip I've made dozens of times over the years: in canoes, motor-boats, catamarans, even on a wooden raft. Something has me thinking that today's outing will be a tad different.

We drag our kayaks through three inches of snow and line them up on the beach, just out of wave's reach. Some-body mentions that once we leave the bay it's going to get a whole lot rougher, and with that I notice a first twinge of nerves. I'll be using one of David's extra kayaks, a long, nar-row, bound-to-be-tippy thing, yellow as a ripe banana. I'm told that it's got a tight hatch—an "ocean hatch"—which means that if I flip I'll have to really work myself free. "You won't just fall out," David says. "But don't worry, it's easy, like pulling down a pair of trousers."

The day is breathtaking—sunny, almost cloudless, sharp. Sure, it's the kind of day, the kind of sharpness, that makes you wish you didn't have toes or a nose, but still, it's swell to be outside. The guys help me into my ride, secure my skirt, and push me off with a mix of encouraging comments and grim jokes. I practice in the shallows, rocking my hips, try-ing to determine how tippy the banana will actually be. An-swer: very tippy. Like pulling down a pair of trousers, I tell myself. No problem. No big deal.

The shoreline around Kingsland Bay is rugged with rock. Single file, we glide past ledgy walls decorated by ice: rib-bons of ice, flowing curtains of ice, stalactite-icicles barring caves where the water slurps and sloshes, funky crystal ici-cle-chandeliers drooping from overhanging cedars. Ducks fly before us, snapping their wings fast and hard. A bald eagle soars high overhead. I'm thrilled, awestruck, twisting and turning to take it all in. I know that excitement leads to the jitters, the jitters to flipping, flipping to the dreaded Trouser Situation, but I can't help myself.

"Maybe talk to somebody if you get nervous, take your mind off it," Wylie says, floating beside me. He tells me that he's got his roll pretty dialed and even knows how to bend forward while inverted, should he lose his paddle, and grab the extra one strapped to the top of his kayak, then roll up. If he ever needs to wet exit, he's got a pump stowed on board and can drain his craft while swimming next to it, then straddle the back and scoot his way forward to the hatch. "It's good to have lots of ways to solve problems out here," he says. David slips in close, adding that, in general, they try to avoid problems in the first place. Righty-o, very good sir. Avoiding problems. I like.

Shortly, we're rounding leftward into the open lake, abandoning the bay's protection and any chance of further conversation. Miles of whitecaps drive from the north-west—lifting me, dropping me, throwing water across my bow. The waves tackle the cliffs with linebacker force and reflect against themselves, rendering the surface an ugly, incomprehensible mishmash. Trying to read his boat's jumps and twitches, I follow Wylie as he battles even farther out. Cleaner water? Nope. Total chaos. I'm not a particularly wimpy fellow, but this is without a doubt the tensest thing I've done in a long, long time.

Then the tension intensifies. My paddle has accumulated a millimeter-thick coating of ice and wants to slide out of my hands, which also are coated. Worse, my skirt is freezing into place, the Trouser Situation escalating into a bona fide Trouser Emergency. Spray whips my face. I blink. I brace. I focus with the discipline of an almost-to-enlightenment monk. Of course, this is only an amateur's experience, a newbie's fear. Tom and Don are at the base of the cliffs, rollicking in the ruckus, playing around, practicing their rolls, coming up dripping in the sun. Watching them out of the corner of my eye, I feel both inspired and horrified.

We regroup after the worst of it, rafting up by grabbing each other's paddles, then release and keep going in the direction of Fort Cassin and Otter Creek, the water slowly calming around us. The Frostbiters, I'm told, usually do early-season trips near the Champlain Bridge, and they count on late season water around Burlington, where the lake is twelve miles wide. They've also paddled Lake George in New York, and once, everything frozen solid, they drove to Montreal and kayaked the Saint Lawrence River.

"When it's thin, the ice makes a nice tinkling sound around your boat as you break through," David says. I ask about icebergs. "Sometimes, if I need to stretch my legs, I'll run straight at a sheet and slide onto it, get out, make tea on a portable stove, drift around for a while, then gear up at the edge and shoot right back in." I tell him that this has been a lifelong fantasy of mine, to shipwreck myself on an ice-island, a thermos of hot cocoa near at hand.

We scan: luminous water in all directions.

"Not today," he says.

❆ ❆ ❆

Eventually the wind mellows to almost nothing and we make the crossing without difficulty. My feet are cold, my hands coming and going. I'm by no means comfortable, but as long as I keep moving, keep paddling hard, it's not that bad, definitely no worse than being stuck on a stalled ski lift in a blizzard at four thousand feet. Years ago I worked a season in Antarctica, shoveling snow at the South Pole. Frostbiting recalls those days of frigid toil, though it's wetter and more fun.

Over at the Palisades, the coast is peaceful and still, a pocket of ease. A peregrine falcon arcs out, circles, returns to a snag protruding from a shelf 150 feet up. Cracks and steep gullies in the cliff, crammed with ice, run straight to the black water. David goes in close and gets plinked with some loose, falling stuff—little flakes and chips released by the day's gradual warming. Then a dinner plate of crust comes sailing and he gets the heck away. The armada bobs at a distance, necks craned.

In a cove a bit farther south, somebody proposes lunch. A crescent of pebbly beach slicker than a hockey rink offers a landing of sorts. Extracting ourselves—and "extracting" is undoubtedly the right word—is a major production. Like the beach's pebbles, we're encased in ice. I punch my spray skirt with a heavy fist, punch it twenty more times, then work it loose. It's a good sweaty fight, but thanks to some helping hands I'm eventually able to get free.

Once free, though, I chill fast. Standing in knee-deep

snow, eating chili from a Tupperware, my teeth chatter around the spoon. I do funny shifty-dances, knocking my neoprene booties together to keep the blood flowing, and lie to myself that these efforts aren't entirely futile. Nobody talks much. A chocolate bar makes the rounds in silence. "Normally, we don't stop at all, just snack in the boats," David says, and I think I pretty much understand why. Then the meal comes to an end and I *really* understand why.

If getting out of the kayaks was a production, getting back in is a full-blown cryogenic disaster. David, his mittens totally stiff, asks Tom for some of the hot water in his thermos. "That's my hot chocolate, damn it," Tom yells in mock outrage. "You want me to pour my hot chocolate into your mitts? I'm planning on drinking it!" My mitts are also unyielding. Taking a cue from Cathy and Wylie and Don, I do the unthinkable—I tenderize them with a soak in the shallows. The skirts are just as bad, so in they go as well, which means in *we* go, all of us wading around, splashing, kneading our neoprene. This astounds me: a winter sport where the warmest place is *in* the lake.

Minutes pass and I'm still struggling, struggling, struggling with my gear. Picture the pain and frustration of cramming a foot down into an alpine ski boot, now make that foot your entire body and multiply the pain by, say, infinity. Loony with desperation and a still half-exposed hand, I burst out laughing. David is in up to his sternum, pulling with every muscle to help get Tom's skirt over the hatch. The cove is a chorus of groans and whines, heavy breathing and dirty words escaping through clenched jaws. I feel as though my hand could detach. And shatter. So much for that pocket of ease, I guess.

Finally secured in his kayak, Tom howls gleefully in my direction: "A New Year's Day tradition I'll never take part in again, eh?" This triggers a vigorous wisecracking session, everybody chiming in with a personal take on the miseries of Frostbiting. Underneath the self-deprecation and feigned bitterness, though, one can't help but sense a certain quirky pride. The Frostbiters draw energy from the fact that their chosen sport is weird and harsh, its rewards hard-earned. They like that the beauty of the lake at these times, afternoons when water and rocks and ice are glossed with a bronze light, when the sky is a clear, deep, heart-wrenchingly pure blue—they like that this beauty is a secret, esoteric, only-for-the-initiated kind of thing.

Ah, to find another world hidden in the world you know—to feel as if you're off the coast of Labrador or Greenland or Svalbard, where a seal could rise beside your boat, where an indigenous hunter with a harpoon could chase that seal, where an iceberg could invite you onboard for a journey to . . .

Enough! Now's no time for such whimsical reflections. At home tonight, safe and dry, nursing hot toddies by the fire, *then* I'll ponder the art of finding polar-style adventure in cozy, cute Vermont. For the moment, I've got more pressing concerns. Like this mitten. Like getting back into those sketchy "trousers." Like that north wind just beginning to prick the lake.

"A Miskell wind," David says, emerging from the water,

turning to ice before my eyes. "In my honor, that's what these jokers call a wind that kicks up out of nowhere and smashes you in the face, turning with you, always managing to keep right there in your face, making your life miserable."

He smiles—that cheery, scuba-diving Santa Claus smile.

And then, as promised, the waves are huger than huge and I am, once again, euphorically terrified for my shivering life.

A Grebe to Save Our Souls

I'm peering through the car's frosted windshield, into a morning that still looks and feels like night. Up ahead, a café stands out from a row of closed shops and sleepy apartments, as if the whole of town were a single dark house, the lights left on in this one room. I park the car and step out, my breath rising cloudy before my face.

Inside, some twenty men and women, mostly older than middle-aged, are drinking coffee and nibbling muffins, chatting. The room has the snug, sociable vibe of a ski lodge, except instead of goggles everybody's wearing binoculars. Count compiler Mike Winslow stands just inside the door, dressed in a flannel shirt, wool pants, and red suspenders. Part Master of Ceremonies and part Human Bird Calculator, he's responsible for organizing us volunteers, and also for pulling together our findings at the end of the day and reporting them to the Audubon Society's national headquarters. With a firm handshake and a smile that defies the early hour, he welcomes me to the fifty-first Ferrisburgh Christmas Bird Count.

Though I'm a CBC rookie, I've done some research and know what to expect. In a few minutes we'll trade this cozy breakfast for a dozen hours outdoors, our eyes and ears trained on hedges, power lines, bird feeders, riverbanks, and the open sky. A circle measuring fifteen miles in diameter has been mapped onto the local landscape, and it's our job to identify and enumerate all the birds within it. There are twenty of these circles in Vermont, over two thousand of them across the continent. The data collected in each circle helps scientists and conservationists gauge the status, long-term health, and range shifts of avian populations. It's a big project with a rich history. Around sixty thousand birders will be participating in this, the 111th CBC.

Taking a seat across from a man with a long white beard, I ask him, "So how many years does this make for you?" He chews his lips, unresponsive, and for a second I think maybe his coffee hasn't kicked in yet. Then his head snaps up: "I've lost track."

The response strikes me as ironic—this is a bird *count*, isn't it? A year ago today, seventy-one species and 13,097 individuals were observed in the Ferrisburgh circle. The one thing everyone in this room has in common, besides a devotion to their feathered neighbors, is a desire to top last year's numbers. They want bigger numbers because that means healthier bird populations, but the sheer challenge of finding the birds is a motivating factor as well. Tabulating the sightings isn't just science—it's scorekeeping.

My new white-bearded pal is focusing intently on the tabletop again, searching his memory for the lost years, or so it seems. A woman sitting beside him leans toward me and says, "He's an accountant and won't give you a number unless it's exact." Reassured, I chuckle. And already it's time to go.

⁂ ⁂ ⁂

7:46 A.M. Twenty-five degrees. I'm riding shotgun beside Steve Antell, a quiet, meticulous birder from Shelburne who will be my guide and partner for the day. He hits the brakes, pulls to the shoulder, and lifts binoculars, all in one fluid motion. "Red-tail," he says, leaning into the dash, following a dark shape across the sky. I put a third mark on the tally sheet in my lap. He scans the fields around us for another minute before easing the car back onto the road. Average CBC cruising speed is fifteen miles per hour.

Fifty feet off the back bumper, eighty-two-year-old Dick Reid follows with his daughter Jessie and her husband Jeffrey. (Unsurprisingly, Dick's spent an extra couple of bucks for the license plate with the picture of the peregrine falcon.) The Ferrisburgh circle is split into eleven territories, and generally the same group handles the same territory each year. This is Dick's eleventh year covering the Lake Champlain coast in Charlotte, and Steve's thirtieth. They know the area intimately and have designed the morning's route to cover a spectrum of habitats, each home to a different assemblage of species.

We drive for twenty minutes, stopping every half mile or so to bird from the car—*two white-breasted nuthatches behind that mailbox; another tree sparrow; chickadees, five of them*—eventually parking at a private residence bordering an open cove. "Anything with water is likely to be interesting," Steve says, setting up his spotting scope and turning it to a raft of ducks a hundred yards out. Lakefront property is as desirable in winter birding as it is in real estate, providing access to a host of floaters that won't be found inland on frozen creeks and ponds. The Ferrisburgh circle includes many miles of jigsaw coast and routinely reports more species than any other circle in the state.

While Steve counts ducks, Jeffrey pokes around a corner, searching a marsh for blue herons, and Jessie picks two bald eagles out from a cottony cloud. Dick and I stand beside each other, holding our hats against a head-on wind, debating whether a buoy is in fact a seagull. "It's like the old saying," he jokes, face literally frozen into a smile: "'You don't have to be crazy, but it helps.'"

Back at the car an hour later, Steve emphasizes that this isn't hard science, but citizen science. Our goal is to paint a picture of avian populations with broad brushstrokes, to gain in coverage at the expense of precision. The fact that an individual bird gets missed or counted twice, or that a particularly animated buoy might find its way into the data set, is not just an accepted part of the process—it's part of the fun. Hence a morning of humor.

"Hey, how'd you get that 12,681 Canada geese?"

"Oh, it was easy. I was estimating in groups of 12,681, so I said, 'That's one.'"

⁂ ⁂ ⁂

Lunch is a buffet at another volunteer's house: mugs of chili followed by brownies, wet cuffs and floppy wool socks in abundance. Dick's sipping a coffee, saying something—perhaps in earnest, perhaps in jest—about positive thinking and *willing* the birds. A young man and woman who covered the southern part of our territory are going over some of their finds with Steve, describing exactly where they went and what they saw. There's a meditative calm to bird-watching, to bestowing one's complete attention on the beauty and mystery of another life, but as with any focused activity, the task is tiring. It feels good to sit back and relax the ornithological awareness for a while, to let the mind wander other realms.

Back in the late 1800s many nature lovers participated in a not-so-quaint Christmas tradition known as the Side Hunt. Two heavily armed teams would enter the woods around town, and the team that returned with the most feathered and furred carcasses was deemed the winner. Wildlife conservation was still a relatively novel idea in 1900 when Frank Chapman, an officer of the fledgling Audubon Society, replaced the guns with binoculars for the first-ever CBC.

I'm thinking about this, about how glad I am to be watching birds rather than shooting them, and on top of that how glad I am to be warming my toes, when a white flock swoops past a bay window, glittery against a brownish hill. The room erupts into commotion, everyone rushing to the glass—*what's that, snow buntings, how many?* I pop a last bite of brownie into my mouth, wondering if maybe it wasn't a flock of huge snowflakes swept up by the wind. Perhaps we should make more coffee before filing out to investigate, maybe even take a quick nap? Steve runs to get his binoculars, which can mean only one thing: lunch is officially over.

⁝ ⁝ ⁝

Birds are morning people; they don't much like these copper rays slanting low through the skeleton trees. I guess the same can be said for Jessie and Jeffrey, because they quit after lunch, Dick an hour after them. Most of the major sites and species accounted for, Steve and I tour opportunistically, swinging behind tire-covered manure stacks to add a third digit to our pigeon count, edging our way out to the tip of Long Point just in case something's doing. An excited fellow comes out of his house—he participated in the CBC years ago, in the Midwest—and birds at our side. A juvenile goshawk has been dropping by in the afternoons, he says, so we wait around, but it never shows.

Done for the day and yet still on duty (the Ferrisburgh counting period will conclude at midnight), we pull over a last time. Three hairy woodpeckers climb a maple's grooved trunk, red caps like strawberries, patterned backs reminding me of skunks. We stand in the quiet road, watching. Neither Steve nor I have ever seen three hairy woodpeckers together at the same time before. It's a small wonder, one of a hundred knit into the fabric of what's been a long and satisfying day.

Come four o'clock, Steve and I part ways with a gloved handshake. He says he'll total our results and email them to me within the hour, then I can go to the potluck dinner and report them to the group.

"You're not coming?" I ask.

"I've got a date with my hot tub."

‡   ‡   ‡

Town is dark again when I park behind the Congregational Church and head for the basement entrance. Through a ground-level window Mike Winslow and his red suspenders stand out. In a long, low room, many of the faces from breakfast, along with a handful of new ones, lean over tally sheets. Tables loaded with salads, breads, casseroles, and desserts line the walls. A woman who must be in her nineties sits surrounded by friends.

Mike greets me and describes the evening's feature event. "Once we get settled, I'll ask who's seen a chickadee, or some other very common bird, and everyone will raise a hand. Then I'll bump it up to something less common, like a Carolina wren. Then I'll ask if anyone's got anything left." A smile, the same smile that greeted me early this morning, spreads across his face. "That's when you play your hand."

Play my hand? I peruse the printout Steve sent me and try to decide what's more impressive, a red-necked grebe or a gadwall. "Don't tell anybody your birds until I ask for them," Mike says with the friendly, fatherly tone of a T-ball coach. A gray-haired woman in a heart-patterned sweater overhears and comes up close to my ear. "Oh, c'mon," she says, feigning the silky, whispered voice of seduction. "You can tell *me* your birds."

Wine's flowing from a box and the chow is good. Mike starts the compiling by opening it up to nonbird highlights—*we saw the most beautiful bobcat; an eight-point buck, close as that table; two otters pulling up fish and throwing them against the ice.* Then it's on to the Aves. The first round yields some impressive numbers: 3,305 starlings, 1,007 goldeneyes, 255 wild turkeys. Numbers are slimmer in the second round, but comedy fills the gaps.

"Any song sparrows?"

"Two and three-quarters."

"Two and three-quarters?"

"Well, he was a little round bugger without a tail."

Forty minutes in we've covered the obvious species and already added a few more. Last year's record of seventy-one surpassed, the game for bragging rights begins. "Any other ducks?" Mike asks, and the room goes silent. "How about a northern shrike?" No one says anything. "A red-necked grebe?" Mike swivels, beseeching us with that smile of his. I check my list, not wanting to blow it, and slowly raise my hand.

"Where?" a mustachioed guy sitting next to me cries, his voice raised above the din of applause, his eyes sparkling like Christmas lights. "We couldn't find a grebe to save our souls!"

⸭ ⸭ ⸭

10:33 P.M. Nine degrees. I'm at home, sunk in quilts, moonlight beaming through the window. In four short hours I'll rise to meet Mike Winslow and do some owling for the Middlebury count. (The CBC spans the weeks around Christmas and New Year's Eve, different circles in different parts of the state surveyed on different days). We'll broadcast hoots into inky woods from portable speakers, then wait, perfectly still, our ears pricked to the night's faint sounds. When the sun rises we'll meet many of the folks from the Ferrisburgh count at a diner on Route 7. As a group, we'll eat and talk and prepare for another dozen hours in the field. From Alaska to Texas to Ontario to Florida, thousands of groggy but eager birders will be doing the same.

For now, though, I'm happy to be lying here, thinking about hummingbirds. On cold nights, hummingbirds fall into a coma-like state to conserve energy, then shiver themselves awake with the dawn. Scientists aren't sure what triggers the shivering; they assume it has to do with circadian rhythms, that in some deep way the birds just know.

During the Vermont winter, it's not uncommon for us humans to inhabit our own torpid worlds. The question is: what will wake us up? Today I saw one option. There at the end of my binoculars' dark tunnel, I saw the polished beaks and delicate wings that draw us out of ourselves, into a deeper relationship with the landscape. I saw a community of people who roll out of bed at an ungodly hour without questioning why. It's the CBC. It's that simple. Grab your coffee and go.

A blue rectangle of moonlight imprints the bedspread. Wind rushes the windowpanes. At the border of sleep, I wait for merinos, for fleecy jumping sheep, and instead find birds—not hummingbirds, but winter birds, Vermont birds, one perched after another on fences, feeders, and branches loaded with snow.

The Smiles Are Huge

Lee Wiseman is a family friend and connoisseur of "weird outdoor things" who lives on a forested hill in a back corner of Charlotte. Seven years ago, in his driveway, I first rode a jack jumper. It was a typical winter morning: overcast, chilly, the week-old snow between the pine's trunks flecked with fallen needles. Lee led me to a shed where his jack jumper hung from a beam. He lowered it with both hands, as one might a delicate artifact from a display case, and we crunched out to the snow-packed drive.

Like all jack jumpers, Lee's was homemade. A single Dynastar ski scavenged from the factory dumpster. A twelve-inch steel post with welded support braces mounted on the ski where the binding would normally go. A plywood bench atop the post, covered in foam and canvas, large enough for a medium-sized backside. It was an odd-looking contraption, yet perfectly simple. In fact, it was *beyond* simple. The thing was honest, refusing to hide its cobbled-togetherness behind a fancy paint job or sleek, molded plastics. Lee set it at our feet, and we both stared for a moment in the sharp gray light.

My first run was wobbly and slow, reminiscent of early

attempts to ride a bike without training wheels. Lee pointed out two garage door handles screwed to the underside of the seat, explaining that if you pull up against these and lean into your turn the jack jumper is as responsive as skis or snowboard. He told me that I could ride with my feet lightly touching the ground, or, if my balance permitted, I could extend my legs in front of me, as if sitting on the floor with my back to a wall. I took four runs, the last of which was my best. It lasted five seconds and ended in a snowbank.

Since that day in the driveway I've logged more hours of mountain elation on a jack jumper than on any other of winter's beloved snow-sliding devices (this coming from a cold-weather sports enthusiast with decades of alpine, telemark, and Nordic skiing experience, not to mention a committed, almost freakish passion for sledding the Green Mountains' hiking trails). Yes, the ride is thrilling, fluid, and fast—close, I'm tempted to say, to what I imagine birds and fish feel when they so gracefully cut through fields of sky and water. The serenity and wholesomeness of afternoons spent hiking up and riding down winding, unplowed gap roads in the company of friends and quiet mountains and a million snowflakes' slow-motion drift—yes, that's a part of jack jumping's allure as well. But there's something beyond even these, beyond the act itself. A ski and a seat. A Vermont pastime that predates the T-bar. When jack jumping, we come to know our place in a rich folk tradition, and we enjoy the knowing.

⁂

Bound by no official, written history, jack-jumping creation stories mix fact, rumor, and imagination. "I can't prove this academically," Lee said to me when I phoned him last winter to discuss the finer points of our shared hobby, "but jack jumping is in the lineage of a uniquely Vermont pursuit." A few reports of something jack jumper–like have come out of Michigan now and then over the years, and in one of the Beatles' movies the four boys ride some Swedish seat-ski things. Nobody I've talked to has seen jack jumpers in New Hampshire or the Adirondacks, though, and a friend from Jackson Hole just laughs when I mention introducing the sport to the Rockies.

Jack jumping's "mythic origin," as Lee calls it, harks back to a time when roads were rolled rather than plowed and Vermonters knew nothing of ski resorts, deafening snow-cannons, or hip-baggy snow pants. Mark Stirewalt, a hardcore jumper from Waterbury who once descended the Tuckerman's Ravine headwall on Mt. Washington ("Blink, it was over") has one jack jumper from the 1920s; its narrow ski, though useless in powder, would have been perfect for roads packed hard by the passage of horses and sleighs. Silas Towler, a friend of Lee's who lives in North Ferrisburgh, had an old farmer-neighbor named Roy Higbee who jack jumped as a kid around the turn of the century. Roy's jack jumper—built by his father, a man who was possibly exposed to jack jumpers in his own childhood—represents the iconic historical image: its single ski was fashioned from a barrel stave, its wooden seat handcrafted.

Most folks agree that jack jumpers are a product of Vermont farm life—"a toy to while away the long winter days," as Silas puts it—but that doesn't stop alternative stories from taking hold of those who ride certain hills or live in certain valleys. Some say loggers used to jack jump skid roads as a quick way of exiting the woods after exhausting sessions sawing. Others say jack jumping is an art mastered by early lift mechanics and snowmakers, ski resort employees who didn't own skis but still needed to move efficiently within a mountain's network of trails. In the end, there's doubtless no single origin, no one locale or personality responsible for this classic Vermont pastime. Jack jumpers have never been successfully marketed, mass-produced, or homogenized, and the sport's stories are the same, springing up here and there, created in one barn workshop or another. Even the name's a mystery: *who's Jack?*

⁞ ⁞ ⁞

The morning after my first driveway ride, just before seven, I returned to Lee's house accompanied by my friend Craig. His brother had recently assembled a jack jumper, and being the outdoorsy, athletic, curious fellow that he is, Craig promptly heisted it. Like me, he'd not yet ridden anything longer or steeper than a driveway. With Lee's blessing I popped into the shed, and minutes later Craig and I were charging rough, frost-split roads en route to Mt. Ellen, two borrowed jack jumpers chattering around behind us in the truck's bed.

It was a postcard kind of day in the high hills, clean and

bright. Craig and I wore torn snow pants, leather work boots, and pigskin gloves. One of us probably sported a woolen cap with floppy earflaps, basset hound–style. Approaching the lift at the base of the bunny slope, jack jumpers slung over our shoulders in the manner of those bindles hobos used to carry, we must have looked less like Sugarbush Resort patrons than like the guys there to shovel the walk.

Though I'd skied Sugarbush for years, I'd never gone anywhere near the bunny slope. I'd also never strolled onto the loading deck, waited for the chair to swing around, and reclined with a hunk of metal, wood, and ski in my lap. Our unencumbered feet dangling and kicking as we ascended, Craig and I discussed the impending catastrophe: offloading. Lee had recommended "The Superman." Right when you'd normally plant your poles, stand up, and push, he said, just set the jack jumper's ski to the snow, belly flop onto the seat, and ride away head first. To our surprise, when the time came we slid down the ramp as naturally as two otters would a bank. We coasted over to the top of the trail, hitched dog leashes around our ankles, and clipped them to our jack jumpers' metal frames in compliance with resort safety regulations. We knew that aside from Mt. Snow, which hosts a dual slalom race one day a year, only Sugarbush, Bolton Valley, and Jay Peak allowed jack jumpers.

As with riding a bike, one needs speed to balance a jack jumper. Conservative as we were with gravity's great pulling power, it took a long first run of veering, teetering, and crashing onto our hips to learn this. Craig and I like speed, though, and by ten that morning we were hammering blue squares, by noon groomed black diamonds. Sometimes we rode with only one hand holding on, the other arm outstretched like a wing. Sometimes we got caught in moguls and bucked from our seats. At the mountain's summit, prepared to run a few thousand uninterrupted vertical feet to the lodge, we took a moment to relax our adrenal glands. Much of Vermont's rumpled topography was visible out beneath the sky's endless azure, a thousand hollows and hills where unseen jack jumpers—both the people and the things—were at rest, or at play.

Silas: "It's a fantasy." Lee: "It's a gas." Craig hollered some exclamations of delight and appreciation that probably aren't fit for print. Because your center of gravity is so low on a jack jumper, the carving is unreal. Because one ski generates less friction than two, the speed is unparalleled. Because you're wearing work clothes, you're comfortable. Because you're sitting down, you hardly need to rest. Like the runs and like the seasons, the "becauses" go on and on. I'll only mention one more. Because you know you are a small part of a long tradition, and that you are maintaining that tradition in the face of a perpetually advancing culture obsessed with the new, the different, and the cutting-edge, because of this the runs feel longer somehow, as if they extend backward and forward through time.

⁂

We rode from opening to closing, thirty descents, each linked to the next in a sequence uninterrupted by warming huts or hot chocolate. Near the end of the day I pulled to the side of the trail and waited for Craig to crest a steep pitch beneath the lift line. He came sweeping into view like he was riding some kind of rocket-booster chair—and I heard someone yelling. Above me, a boy, maybe eleven years old, waved his hands and wiggled in his seat. "Awesome!" he shouted, head rotating on his shoulders like an owl's to keep Craig's descent in view. But Craig was already gone, and I was laughing into my collar, smiling a smile nobody would ever see.

Reflecting on what I hope is only the short beginning of a long jack-jumping life, I think of that inspired kid, and I recall something Mark Stirewalt, the guy who jumped Tuck's, kept saying to me on the phone last winter. It wasn't so much a point he was making as it was a punctuation, a simple statement welling up from some place inside him that is also inside me—a few words to give our discussion pause. We were speaking of jack jumpers, their designs, their satisfactions, and what it takes for a little-known form of outdoor recreation to survive from generation to generation. "The smiles are huge," Mark would say, and I'd say, *Yeah, huge*, and the conversation would roll on from there.

And then again, five minutes later: "The smiles are huge."

Spandex and Firepower

I prepared for my first-ever biathlon race by drinking coffee until noon, skipping lunch, and getting myself good and emotionally disheveled during a phone conversation with my long-distance girlfriend. At some particularly intense moment in that conversation, realizing that I was running late, I blurted out that I needed to hang up right away in order to make the 5:30 firearm safety session (mandatory for newbies like myself) that precedes the 6:30 start. Glory was most decidedly not in the cards, but still, I had to go.

Figuring that the other racers would look the part in intricately patterned spandex jumpsuits and tight woolen skullcaps, I threw open my closet door. Floppy orange hunting hat and tie-dyed union suit, saggy in the backside? That outfit seemed a bit off the mark, and biathlon is, of course, fundamentally concerned with marksmanship. Bulky ski pants, a sweater, a raincoat, and a pair of thin fleece gloves would have to suffice. I ran for the door, turned around, grabbed a hunk of cheddar cheese from the fridge, and ran again, this time right on out to the car, straight past my skis.

About that. I grew up on antique-y hand-me-downs, wooden plank-like things you might see hanging above the hearth at a rustic lodge. Three-pin boots. Bamboo poles. A network of narrow, winding, ungroomed trails cut into the forest behind my grandfather's house. My experience as a cross-country skier has seen me atop boulders, at the edge of remote beaver ponds, even towed behind a snowmobile by a length of old rope, but never on a racecourse, and certainly not on sleek, fancy skate skis (I've always skied "classic," the form associated with NordicTrack machines). I'd talked with a friend, though, an ex-racer and part-time college coach, and he'd emphasized that skating—dig in with both poles, push off from the inside edge of the right ski, coast forward on the left, switch sides and repeat—was the biathlon norm.

I hurried over to this friend's house, where he had everything waiting: two skis, each about an inch wide; two plastic boots, each with a drawcord, buckle, *and* zipper; and two long fiberglass poles, each featuring a complex holster strap that fits around your hand. Back in the car, I sped through the early dark night of Hinesburg, Richmond, and Jericho. How I managed to notice the sign on the Jericho town green commemorating Snowflake Bentley, pioneer snow crystal photographer of yesteryear, but miss the much larger sign that I was after, is a mystery attributable only to my extreme lack of prerace composure. I pulled a U-turn and caught the sign the second time around—Vermont National Guard, Camp Ethan Allen Training Site.

I wondered, Do they make camouflage spandex?

⁕ ⁕ ⁕

Biathlon is, and always has been, a military sport. Formal competitions date back to the Great Scandinavian War of 1700–1718 (though one not necessarily credible website I found presents the cool anthropological hypothesis that the sport's roots lie in ancient winter hunting traditions). In the United States, biathlon calls to mind the Tenth Mountain Division and commandos on skis. But in 1973, the "biathlon mission"—the maintenance of training facilities and the coaching of athletes for World Cup– and Olympic-level competition—was transferred from the regular army over to the National Guard. The Ethan Allen Training Facility, as it turns out, hosts some very important national and international races and has provided a base for more than a handful of the sport's aspiring and established stars. Though I didn't know it at the time, I was heading for the big leagues (sort of).

I drove past barracks covered with snow, a wooden climbing structure like you see Marines dragging themselves over in television ads, and lots and lots of fences. One fence blocked my path—Authorized Personnel Only, Keep Out—but that was just another wrong turn. Though the Ethan Allen Training Facility is not open to the public, the Vermont National Guard, in a gesture of Nordic goodwill, permits local high school teams and ski clubs to practice and race on their course. In a parking lot beside a forest illuminated by tree-mounted floodlights, a school bus nearly backed into me. *Whoa there, pal!* I took a deep breath, gnawed my block of cheddar, and laced-buckled-zippered my boots. Then entered the pain.

"Stabbing" is a useful word, but "spirit-goring" is perhaps a more accurate way of describing the violent gusts in Jericho that evening. And it wasn't just wind, but ice as well: ice on the parking lot, ice on the groomed corduroy racecourse, ice on the steps leading up to the shed that serves as a warming hut and check-in station. Slipping on those steps and banging my elbow wasn't exactly the confidence-boosting introduction to biathlon that I needed, but what can you do?

Inside: "Hi, I've never biathloned, or raced it, or, um, I don't know how you say it, but I'd like to race it, or...You know what I mean." I paused to gather my words. "That is, I'm ready to make a fool of myself."

A grandmotherly woman sitting beside a box of bibs, taking names and stacking ten-dollar bills (entry fees), handed me a waiver that I signed without reading. "Oh, we can make that happen," she said. "This is the iciest we've seen the course in a while." I asked for some background on the race and she told me that it's sponsored by the Ethan Allen Biathlon Club (EABC), a civilian group with about twenty-five permanent members and many more supporters, founded back in 1985. Along with a club out of Craftsbury Common (whose members routinely make the trek to compete in Jericho), the EABC represents the core of biathlon culture in northern Vermont. From late December through February, the EABC hosts a "Thursday Night under the Lights" race series. A few of the National Guard elites race, as do some very serious, fit, talented civilian athletes, as do some midgrade competitors, folks who probably raced straight cross-country (no rifles) in their youth. Newcomers are always welcome, regardless of experience.

"I guess that's me," I said, and thanked her.

Bib pulled on, hood pulled up, I lurched out into the wind, in search of a gun.

§ § §

If biathlon is a body, the shooting range is a brain tying together a web of nerve trails. Said differently: the range is where races are lost and won. At the professional level, the athletes are skiing at basically the same pace. But for every missed shot you have to take a short penalty lap on a little loop just beside the range. One lap and you're done. And so it really does come down to the shooting, not just hitting the targets (because the pros commonly shoot five for five), but the speed with which you can ditch your ski poles, flop onto the ground, load a magazine of five bullets into your rifle, target, fire, repeat four more times, get up, and get out. The pros are done in under thirty seconds.

A man named Tom was waiting for me beside the light-saturated range, a .22 in his arms. He told me that I wouldn't have to worry about skiing with the rifle slung over my back; because most Thursday Night competitors don't own their own rifles (biathlon rifles cost as much as three thousand dollars!), we'd be sharing, a club rifle here for me each time I finished a lap.

After a jargon-heavy firearm crash course that lasted less than a minute and a half, I "got prone" and snugged the gun up against my cheek. The wind was tornadoing ice crystals into my teary-blurry eyes, but the scope on the gun was amazing, so different from old .22s I'd shot at stumps and cans over the years. I squeezed the trigger and—*ping*—a black saucer-sized target fifty meters out flipped over, turning to white. *Ping*—another. *Ping, ping, ping*—I shot five for five. "Are you sure you've never done this before?" Tom asked. I did feel proud, but played it humble, saying that I was interested to see how I'd fare once my heart was exploding, my whole upper body rising and falling with each gulping breath. "Yeah," he nodded. "That's the sport."

My hands were numb from handling the gun in my thin gloves: it was time to learn to skate. About seven awkward glides out from the range I came upon a man in full red jumpsuit, red hat, red balaclava. His style was easy, balanced, graceful, so I asked him for pointers. "Follow your nose," he said, the accent thick, maybe Russian. It seemed like credible life advice in general, and he did appear to be skiing nose-first, like a dog pulled fluidly through the woods by a scent. (I later learned that this Man in Red was a famous coach and Olympic gold medalist.)

In my total ignorance I'd not realized there would be hills on the course, but my brief warm-up ski informed me in all-too-clear terms that—*huff, huff, argh!*—climbing was a major part of the sport. I didn't have the strength to "skate" my way up the hills; instead, I tromped them, duck-footed and always on the verge of tripping. A touch frustrated, I circled back to the firing range. At least I was sweating.

⁂ ⁂ ⁂

There are many ways biathlon can be raced. Tonight we'd ski three two-kilometer laps separated by two sessions at the firing range (like a double-decker sandwich: ski, shoot, ski, shoot, ski), and any penalty laps incurred. We'd begin with a "mass start."

Forty or so racers stood poised in a dense group. I shouldered up to a French guy who'd lived in Vermont for six years and was also new to the sport, though less new than me. "How'd you get into it?" I asked. He said his doctor had recommended he stop alpine ski racing (knee injuries). "I've been reading about meditation," he said, "and how to calm myself at the moment of firing." I mentioned something vaguely Buddhist about single-point focus and intentional breathing, but the Frenchman just blinked at me. Whatever. It was too cold to talk religion anyway. And then we were off.

The start was thrilling—a rushed, energized herd sensation, no stopping, no effort, the skiers in the rear pushing forward, propelling me from behind. By the time I reached the first climb, though, the pack had thinned out, and by the top of that hill I was close to last, not that I cared or actually knew. I couldn't spare the second to glance over my shoulder, busy as I was working my glide and following my nose. Which, incidentally, I kept having to wipe with the back of my hand. Which, connected to my pole by that weird holster thing, made me afraid of punching myself in the face should the pole's tip catch on the snow.

The skiing was fun: fast, rhythmic, icy enough in places to conjure memories of my youthful, edge-of-control skittering on Granddad's adventure trails. The course had the variety needed to keep things interesting—sharp turns, easy flats, dips, dives, bridges, even a few dark corridors lost to the flooding lights. I noticed some of the front runners (folks that had already lapped me) tucking on hills and tried that in imitation, but on the whole I couldn't take too seriously the idea that wind resistance would have any impact on my race results. There was nothing to prove and nothing to lose. I felt the Scandinavian blood pumping in my Irish-Italian temples. I tasted Vermont's hard, sharp air—the air of night, the air of winter—rushing my torn-up lungs.

If the skiing was fun, the shooting was even better, though it did go by in a blur. A blur of complete and utter failure, that is. I arrived at the range and Tom, or maybe it was one of the other volunteers who was tending the guns and supplying ammo, encouraged me to "calm my breath." Easily recommended, you sonofa…I sucked deep while collapsing down, skis still on, poles dangling and jangling, and brought my eye to the sight. Oddly, the targets were jumping and jiving, boogieing. What had been a nice dot within the scope, what had been five for five, was a distant memory, a fantasy, beginner's luck. I squeezed the trigger and somebody said, "You're right on the edge," which was a nice gesture, but ultimately useless. Brass shells kicked into the air. They sparkled in the snow around my face.

No *pings*. No *pings!* That was it. Five penalty laps. My nose felt exhausted at the thought.

⁑ ⁑ ⁑

All in all, I shot one for ten (a success!) and came in second to last. The guy who came in dead last was as green to biathlon as I was, and on top of that he was older and heavy-set (or maybe just wearing a lot of warm layers). Nobody was standing around waiting for us, cheering us on, when we did finally sprint across the finish line. Maybe it was silly of me, but I'd expected a spandexed Olympian to be there with a high five and a "Youda man." In reality, the National Guard racers were already back in their barracks, slippers on and tea kettles whistling. I pictured Tom and Coach Red and the Frenchman and everybody else in their cars, halfway home.

Don't get me wrong: my EABC hosts were jovial and friendly and encouraging. But it's cold out there, and by the time you're done you're exhausted, and you're on a military compound, after all—it's not exactly the place for free-flowing hot toddies and bonfire celebrations. More significantly, I was slow, super slow, a skating turtle, a sloth with poor aim. You race, you sweat, you finish, your sweat freezes, and you leave. I didn't take it personally. Had it been metaphysically possible, I wouldn't have waited around for myself either.

Inside the warming hut, returning my bib, I bumped into the only person around: Dan Westover, Nagano Olympian, course caretaker, biathlon guru. We talked for a while as he cleaned up and turned out the lights. I told him about my difficulties at the firing range and he said, as if it were no wild thing, "You don't train to lower your heart rate. You train to shoot at a high heart rate, literally squeezing the trigger between heartbeats." I've not been able to forget this. It is amazing to me. It encapsulates all of biathlon's precision and control and nose-following perfection. It explains the spandex. It is the essence of *Ping*.

Return to Silver Fields

A man walks through fields like silver oceans of snow, his boots crunching on a crust stronger than his weight, a full moon overhead. He has been watching the weather—the meltings and freezings—for days and weeks, awaiting these conditions. Alone, stopping now and then to listen for long minutes into the night's vast quiet, he hears his own breath, an owl's faraway hoot, a cold-cracked branch in the distance. The man knows these sounds as he knows the moonlit fields; he has lived with these sounds and fields, lived *in* them, for decades. He is a farmer, a naturalist, and an artist—a writer and a roamer. Like his father and his father's father before him, he calls this "wide glittering expanse" his home.

One hundred thirty years pass and another man, a younger man in a busier time, walks the same fields beneath the same moon, his boots crunching on a crust just as hard and smooth and bright. For him, too, these are the fields of his life, the fields that summon him to wandering. He diagonals across one field, pushes through a brushy shelterbelt, steps over train tracks, and enters a second field at the center of which stands an ancient leafless tree. He's

photographed this tree with his mind's eye a hundred times
on a hundred winter tramps, shooting it at dawn and dusk
and midnight, in storms and calms and frigid snaps and everything between. Tonight, the branches are a blue lattice
printed sharply on the snow. Blue ink. Shadows. He listens
to the humming road a mile away and thinks of the man
who walked here when the tree was new.

⁂

The first man, the remembered man, is Rowland Evans
Robinson. He was born in Ferrisburgh, Vermont, in 1833 at
a house named Rokeby, and died there, in a bed in a par-
lor behind the kitchen, in 1900. The house sits in a copse
of maples on a slight rise just east of today's Route 7, the
Champlain Valley's most heavily trafficked road. Fields out
back ease into the low forested ridge of Shellhouse Mountain, where "panthers" once guarded the huckleberry patch
during "huckleberry-time." Fields out front, west of the
road, sweep down to Little Otter Creek and its tributary
slangs, to a marshland bordering Lewis Creek known as Jig-
wallick (an Anglo version of the Abenaki's *chegwalek*—"at
the place of the frog").

Bought in 1793 by Rowland's grandparents, Rokeby has
over the centuries been and become many things, including
a sheep farm, a dairy farm, an orchard, a stop on the Under-
ground Railroad, and a museum commemorating the lives
of four generations of Robinsons. Nowadays, visitors can
tour the grounds, peer into crooked barns, or linger in that
room where Rowland, blinded by age, composed stories

and essays with the aid of a writing board. Gathered around the fireplace, his wife and children would read aloud what he'd written, jotting corrections as he spoke them, preparing his manuscripts for magazines such as *Scribner's, Forest and Stream,* and the *Atlantic Monthly.* Rural life, that's what Rowland knew, and that's what he wrote about.

In the Greenwood. Hunting without a Gun. Uncle Lisha's Outing. Sam Lovel's Camp. A Hero of Ticonderoga. A Danvis Pioneer. Rowland's fourteen books range widely in style, from history lessons to folktales with phonetically spelled dialects to exuberantly recounted nature yarns featuring animals that creep, swim, soar, and burrow. *Silver Fields and Other Sketches of a Farmer-Sportsman,* published posthumously in 1921, is a little-known classic, its title essay a paean to the beauty and power of New England's coldest, sparest months. As with the fields and snow and moon it takes for a subject, it is a shining, timeless thing.

Which brings us to the second man, the man drifting in and out of blue branch-shadows, stamping his feet to keep warm, hooting responses to the owls of his own age even as he tunes his ears to the owls of the past. If you've not already guessed, this man is me. I became him ten years ago. Or maybe I should say I became him *over* the last ten years.

When I was eighteen, my mother moved to a house a mile from Rokeby. Though my childhood home was only one town north, and though I was soon to leave for college in Colorado anyway, I felt the move as an ache in my chest. I'd grown up more out-of-doors than in and was not yet ready to say goodbye to the particular pine stands, mucky gullies, and, yes, cornfields and hayfields that had grounded my life. To make matters worse, my mother was moving to a *neighborhood*, albeit a small one. Having recently read Thoreau's *Walden* for the first time, I was none too pleased by this turn toward civilization.

But what does a college freshman know of blessings in disguise? Back from school on holiday break that first December, snowshoeing beyond the last snug house with its twinkly window-framed Christmas tree, I discovered, to my surprise, the great spacious invitation of the fields—the long blank plains, the huge fresh sky. Barbed-wire fences sifted the wind. Peach-colored clouds went rose with the sunset. Wild turkeys left angelic wing impressions where they had beaten upward into flight. I followed paths—hooks and swerves of nervous mice, a coyote's steady plod—and made my own. I met the ancient tree that would become my friend, returning and returning and returning over the years.

In the fields I encountered a stillness that allowed, or drew forth, a corresponding stillness in myself—a profound peacefulness, you might say. A part of me came to believe that this quality of land and psyche had been around forever, that in some mysterious way the fields and the walking of the fields existed, and would always exist, in a pocket outside time.

And then, browsing a library bookshelf one afternoon, who should I bump into but my old ghost-neighbor from up the way: Rowland, pipe in mouth, smoke curling between us. He reached across the page to shake my hand, asking if I was ready to go.

⚬ ⚬ ⚬

"Silver Fields" begins with a meteorological report both lyrical and precise. Wind directions, specific qualities of rain and sleet and snow, temperatures rising and falling and holding steady—all is recorded with the patience and attentiveness to detail one expects from a farmer-cum-naturalist. "When the full moon comes pulsing up behind the evergreen-crested hill," Rowland writes, "it is no time to bide within doors." The fields crusted to perfection, we're urged to accompany our narrator on his sojourn, to bundle up and brave the elements for the sake of exploration and wonder. It's participatory, a shared outing: "Let us set our faces toward the moon and trail our shadows behind us."

I recall a January night strolling with my sister and her dog, that moon a hole punched from the felty darkness, the snow underfoot softer than Rowland's frozen sheets but no less dazzling. Absentminded, perhaps dazed by the "celestial light" flooding the fields, I made the mistake of letting the dog off his leash. He vanished. A white dog against white. A shadow cast by nothing—a shadow *running*—and then not even that. When at last he turned up an hour later, panting and smiling, I almost tripped on him. He was like a magic trick, like a rabbit pulled from a hat.

So it goes in "Silver Fields." The writing is surreal, a mirror held to a dream. We stalk a fox that turns out to be a stump. The tracks of weasels, skunks, and hares, expanded to five times their size by cycles of thaw and freeze, spark fantasies of giants. Images emerge and disperse, thoughts and landmarks come and go. We're in the fields, then in the cattails by a pond that fractures and booms, then weaving through a maze of trees "that show as plainly as in a summer day." At the cliffy foot of Shellhouse Mountain we pause in awe before an ice cascade: "dull silver, burnished here and there with moon-glint." Little happens on this slow, aimless meander, but much is experienced. A sense of place is enriched with a thousand noticed details. The toes get cold and we float on home.

Since that fateful day in the local library I've made it a habit—no, I've made it a *tradition*—to read "Silver Fields" at least once every winter. Usually, I'll have just concluded a two-hour ramble; more often than not, I'll be wearing flannel pajamas and sipping a mug of herbal tea strengthened with a nip of whiskey. For me, returning to "Silver Fields" is like sharpening the ice skates or shoveling the walk after November's first storm—it's something to anticipate, a simple practice to lead me deeper into the mood of the season.

Kicking back by the fire, the book a blanket in my lap, I picture Rowland just up the road, sitting in that room where he was born and eventually died, a blind man gazing into the dimness of his mind and seeing there the brilliance of the "wide glittering expanse." I picture his hands working over the writing board at some late hour, his family gone to bed, his own fire popping and clicking beside him. He's walking those fields inside his memory, stopping now and then to lean and listen into the night's vast quiet. He's searching for the words that will help a reader 130 years hence feel what he has felt and is feeling now, again.

In my imagination everything comes rushing back: the

smell of spruce and woodsmoke, the faint jingle of sleigh bells, the boot-crunch, the breath-cloud, the stillness like a hand within which all else is cupped. For a moment, I'm bewildered, unsure who's doing the remembering. We brace ourselves against "a cold that no armor of wool or fur can ward off." We cast down "a newly minted coin" to "see how dull a dot it is on the surface." I set the book aside, finish my tea, look out the window at feathers of snow sailing past the porch light. Rowland refills his pipe, settles deeper into his chair, and strikes a match.

⁂

"Silver fields is not a good enough name tonight for these shining farms," my old ghost-neighbor writes in his essay's last paragraph, the tone celebratory, the line twisting language's failure into an ultimate gesture of praise. He knows the impossibility of his task; he knows that no words could ever sparkle as the land has and does and will. And yet he tries. He speaks that less-than-silver name, and for his effort I am grateful.

John Elder, a naturalist and author who operates a sugar bush a few towns east of Ferrisburgh, has written of reading landscapes and hiking through texts. This poetic notion— this blurring of boundaries between literature and elemental earth—has something to do with the way I've deepened my relationship to the Rokeby fields and their human and natural histories. How exactly it all works, though, is beyond my understanding. I only know for certain that over the past ten years, as I've grown into adulthood, the act of

reading and the act of walking have twined themselves together to form for me a life. It's a life that has in turn been
further twined with Rowland Robinson's life and the larger
life of the fields. It's a life that at its best moments is without
margin or boundary, in many places and times at once.

A man steps over train tracks, cuts across crust, presses
his hands to the crystal-frosted trunk of an ancient tree. A
second man, an older man, approaches from a different direction. The men gaze into the crown of twisted branches
and the sharp blue net of shadows. They circle the tree—
once, twice, three times—then walk off together. Nearby
but far away, the humming road goes silent. An owl hoots,
its voice full and round as the moon.

So Gone

The hot months, the green months, the bug-loud months of summer—I don't enjoy these so much as endure them. I was born in December, and winter's cold lives somewhere between my heart and bones. To recall a favorite place is to recall a favorite season, a favorite *place in time*. If you ask me, Little Otter Creek is best explored on a twenty-below evening, the sun dropping orange in the west, the sky purple, a stillness everywhere.

It's not just the mood—that lovely, lonely mood, the breath before your face a drifting screen, coyotes yipping in the distance. Practically speaking, you simply can't access the wetland's secret spots without the help of ice and skates. Each autumn, I pace the creek's sere shore in anticipation, studying the surface on sharp mornings, waiting, watching, feeling pent-up and impatient. Geese cut south overhead. Painted turtles bury themselves in mud. The namesake otters roll and disappear. Then, finally, the wind dies and the temperature falls for three straight days. Once again, like last year and the year before, I'm gone.

Kick, kick.

So gone.

When my mother moved to Ferrisburgh a decade ago, I was less than thrilled. Houses in a row? A neighborhood? You've got to be kidding me. Sure, it was only a dozen houses, and sure, the development was built on an old orchard where the apples and pears continued to thud against the grass. But a neighborhood? Really? Woods-loving teenager that I was—backpacker, burgeoning Thoreauvian—I wanted nothing to do with civilization. Rather, I wanted room to roam, to wander and perhaps get a bit lost. Heck, I wanted to be done with *rooms* altogether.

To my surprise, I found the lostness that I was looking for a mere half mile away—across the field, over the train tracks, over the barbed-wire fence, down through the brush, down the steep bank, down in the ground's low crease. The Little Otter is intricate, fringed with acres of wild marsh. Besides some duck hunters in October and some bass fishermen in flat-bottomed boats come June, it sees and is seen by few humans. Put it this way: I've encountered far more raccoons and turkeys back there than I have fellow skaters.

Every outing is different, every outing alike. It's dusk, the sky purple against the horizon's orange line, the cold burning at my cheeks. I'm shuffling onto black glass in rubber boots, jumping, listening, strange sounds spidering through my ears. My backpack holds a thermos of tea and a pair of hockey skates, nothing else—no headlamp, no cell phone, no leftover thoughts or concerns from the long day of cars and computers, work and talk. I'm sitting on a log, lacing up, yanking and yanking, tightening the skates until they're part of my body. Tightness is speed and speed is what this is all about. Plodding nature walks are well and good—pause often, pay attention—but not tonight. These blades are freshly sharpened and ready for the blur.

Kick, kick.

Blur.

That first winter on the Little Otter was a revelation, an opening of my mind to the watershed and the possibilities of a tailwind-billowed jacket. Beneath the bridge on Little Chicago Road, rapids tumble through a gorge of rotten ice. Four miles north, having bowed left with an oxbow and leaped a pressure crack, a skater stops short where the broadened creek meets Hawkins Bay's violent chop. This is the interface—mashed-up plates and blocks refrozen into a mosaic too dangerous to touch, slopped over by waves. The long view across Lake Champlain to the Adirondacks beyond. The shiver, the spin, the turnaround. The beginning of another homeward push.

Whether alone or with friends, whether under warm sun or night's early stars, I always notice the same giddy buzz up my backbone when I glide and sprint the Little Otter. Would it be trite to call that buzz freedom? Probably so. What, then, to call it? Nose dripping, eyes watering, I glimpse a pale fish under my skates. *Am I swimming?* A great horned owl swoops low and veers away. *Am I flying?* Maybe I'm dreaming, sleeping. Maybe I'm racing the hard liquid floor of my own subconscious. Maybe we don't have the words to describe this kind of experience, this kind of blur.

Okay, fair enough. Open the thermos. Sip the strong tea.

Call it gone, I guess, so gone. Call it right here, once again, like last year and the year before.

Seven Lengths of Vermont

A coyote darted from the fog of my tiredness, crossing Interstate 80 and the headlight beams with the flickering speed of a ghost, a dream, a hallucination. This was somewhere in Indiana, sometime before dawn. I'd been driving close to forty-eight hours, all the way from San Francisco, stopping only for gas stations and a sunrise nap at a Nebraska rest area. Basin after range after basin after range, Salt Lake City's neon glow, cold starry darkness in Wyoming, roadkill stains, big rigs blowing tires, wind turbines rising from Iowa alfalfa—I'd seen some sights, to be sure. But now a specter-coyote? Too damn much. I took the next exit, parked out back of a dumpy motel, and fell asleep in my seat, just another Green Mountain boy headed home after years bumming around the West.

Morning brought filmy skies, pinging rain, and me—where else?—behind the wheel, trapped on the dangerous, efficient, butt-numbing, brain-dumbing freeway, that supreme homogenizer of the American landscape. Why rush three thousand miles across the continent in a single manic burst, neglecting innumerable cultural and natural curiosities en route? Why subject oneself to the achy, boring torture of three days' and nights' solitary confinement in a 1993 four-speed Toyota Tercel, the radio busted? The answer seemed obvious enough at the time, and even more obvious once I'd escaped Cleveland's traffic, crested a ridge beside Lake Erie, and entered the Adirondack's brilliant, prismatic, everywhere-in-an-instant foliage show.

Obvious. I was trying to reach New England before the leaves finished turning. I was trying to witness autumn's turning in my native place. I was trying to align a personal turning—a turning of my life back toward Vermont—with that greater cycle's unpredictable schedule.

Pedal to the metal, as they say.

§ § §

I grew up in the Champlain Basin, its towns and schools, its forests and marshes. Mine was an outdoorsy childhood, untold hours spent skiing, swimming, biking, tromping, climbing trees, eating worms, catching frogs, building forts. The young me was a connoisseur of muck-abouts, a pioneer of teensy-expeditions, a diminutive dude in grass-stained denim roaming a backless backyard. How come backless? Because the lawn pressed up against cornfields, soggy gullies, pine thickets, miles of terrain rumpling toward the bluish bulk of Camel's Hump, third-highest mountain in the state. Because barbed-wire fences are meant for hopping, for snaking beneath. In a word, I grew up exploring.

It probably came as no surprise to my parents when, at the age of sixteen, lacking any previous backpacking experience, some friends and I set out to hike the wooded spine for which our state—*vert mont*—is named. I knew it only as a spontaneous drive then, but in retrospect it's clear that I was looking for a rite of passage, an old-fashioned confrontation with the elemental forces that pervade all earthly locales and can infuse life with meaning, purpose, direction. Moss and rain, rocks and pain, birdsong, exaltation—I touched and was touched by these. When I emerged exhausted at the far end of the Long Trail, 273 miles and twenty-two days after setting out, I was a new man, or a man for the first time.

Skip ahead a handful of years, over trips in Utah's canyons, California's redwood stands, and Wyoming's bear-tracked backcountry. One summer, on a break from philosophy and ecology studies in Colorado, I rowed, sailed, and drifted the length of Lake Champlain on a handmade raft no roomier than a mattress or kitchen table. The raft was many things to me—my floating house, my floating friend—but mostly it was a plain honest seat, some bobbing planks on which I dwelled, week after week, waiting for the lake, the shore, and the sky above to reveal some unknown facet of their collective being. The facet the lake gave me was wavy, fishy, and thunderstormy, drastically different from the arboreal facet offered by the Long Trail.

This focus on facets, on a landscape's countless faces and our ability to turn our own faces toward them, has everything to do with everything. Vermont, like New Hampshire and New Mexico, like Alabama and Alaska, is infinitely complex. You hike its hollows, paddle its ponds, drive to work, or stroll the path to the barn, and each outing presents a refreshment, your sense of things expanding through an endless series of nuanced iterations. As with clouds and waterfalls, you can never pin Vermont down because it is always moving, always morphing, always different than it was the last time you checked in. The seasons change. The ground beneath your feet shifts, heaves, erodes. Something you knew becomes something you could never have imagined.

Not only is the physical Vermont inherently dynamic, but so too is the experience of the observer, the psyche-in-place. Maybe you're ice-skating, sailing, jeeping. Maybe you're crawling, hands-and-knees adventuring. Alone or with companions? As a naturalist, an athlete, a pilgrim? The styles with which we choose to encounter the land are limitless, the mind with which we encounter the land endlessly variable.

Taken altogether, this is my deep and cherished belief, a belief gifted to me during the unfolding of a raft voyage, a rite-of-passage hike, and a free-wandering childhood. It's a belief in the unbounded potential for exploration close to home.

⁂

Some version of this inspired manifesto looped inside the Toyota Tercel—inside me—during the final hours of that transcontinental slog. I crossed into Vermont with a whoop and a little jig of excitement. Soon I could go slow, dig in, atone for the sinful obliviousness the freeway had bred. A strange and exhausting width of the United States was almost complete, a promising engagement almost begun.

The plan was simple. Over the course of twelve months, I aimed to travel the length of Vermont, from Massachusetts to Quebec, or vice versa, seven times via seven different routes. Each excursion would embrace its own idiosyncrasies and thus rejoice in a unique variation. My hope was that by the end of the year, having journeyed a few thousand miles back and forth through the human and more-than-human communities that comprise the state, I'd be able to draw together in consciousness all those disparate lengths, seeing them—*feeling* them, if only for an instant—as parts of a grand unified whole.

Night again. At Fair Haven, I hung a left onto Route 22A and shot north, sticking my nose out the window to inhale the familiar scent of dirt and cows and rain. The leaves were just turning on the trees—I could tell this, even in darkness. By the time I hit Bridport and Addison County, the thrill of return had worn off and the foggy tiredness was back. Night again, yes, and tired again.

Ghost, dream, hallucination: in a coincidence that seemed too improbable to be one, a coyote flickered in the headlights, tawny-gray and fleeting. Adrenaline surged forth from some ancient gland, pouring into my foot and the brake pedal, the scream of tires on pavement rousing me more immediately and violently than any alarm ever had or could. The coyote was gone. My heart was blasting in my chest. I was awake and alert in the land of my birth, ready to observe.

A glimpse. Seven glimpses. A sprawling experiment in local learning. An immersion into the wildly familiar. A tour of the big backyard. Seven glimpses. A glimpse. What fun!

THE HIKE

It's hard to say much about the Long Trail—"Vermont's footpath in the wilderness"—because you can never say enough. You stand at the Canadian border on a damp morning in early October, clothes and food heavy in your backpack. You walk through colored leaves, twisted roots and polished rocks rising up through the soles of your boots, into your achy legs, into your drumming heart and ballooning lungs. The land gets in you, that's what happens, as you get in the land. You climb mountains and more mountains, drink from springs and more springs, watch moths and watch stars. Weather washes your mind. Thoughts move like weather. Sometimes you are happy, sometimes sad, sometimes bored, sometimes a dozen things at once, each nameless in its own nameless way. Finally, when you reach Massachusetts, loose wet snowflakes are falling and the trees are mostly bare. It's the end of the line, first snow of the year.

What summary could ever do justice to these 273 miles, to an experience so varied and vast, so rich and enriching? Better we put our heads in the ground, stuff our mouths with earth, be grateful in silence. The Long Trail is what Aristotle would call "an animal a thousand miles long." We can focus on pieces of the animal at any given moment, but never on the whole. Likewise, we can talk about the fabulous specimen, about those bits of body we've encountered—the summit of Mt. Mansfield during moonrise, the Clarendon Gorge high with flood, the scampering chipmunk, the decayed stump—but never will we speak truthfully of *the thing itself.*

This Long Trail is huge, powerful, overwhelming. It's a beast whose back I've roamed.

Ten years after my first outing—after losing and locating my teenage self in the animal's intricacies—I hiked the trail again. Southbound. Twenty days. A week of drizzle, a week of gold light, a week of bony cold. But there I go already, reducing the irreducible, the animal 273 miles long, to direction, duration, and a meteorological report. It's hard not to describe my trek this way, and yet it's unfair. Hunched at my desk, caught between ceiling, floor, and walls, countless images come back to me, each an anecdote linked to some precise point on the map, some minute or hour. These images coat the surface of consciousness like leaves papering the surface of a puddle. I search for a theme or pattern that will turn the leaves into a coherent story, but find nothing.

People say this world is made of stories. Wrong. This world is made of world, no more or less. And so the leaves rest on the puddle, beautiful and random, floating, layered in place.

⁂

Oct. 1. I've climbed from the hardwoods to a narrow ridge that climbs higher still, vanishing in mist. This is the spruce-fir zone, all murky-green, all bog-wet, all humming with quiet. My face is turned to the trail, as it has been for hours and will be for hours. Footwork is hard work, tricky and mesmerizing. I feel drugged with the repetition of step-step, breath-breath. In my ears there's only the beat of this walking. The land has contracted around my focus.

Whump-whump-whump-whump-whump. A ruffed grouse in rusty plumage fires out from the drooping ferns inches to my right. The grouse's wingbeats—so much louder than anything else in this subdued forest—break through my hypnosis, stopping me in my tracks. For a second I'm terrified, like I've woken, disoriented, from the thickness of dream. I look around. Already the grouse is absent, but my awareness is up. Other birds appear among the trees: blue jays, black-capped chickadees, white-breasted nuthatches, golden-crowned kinglets. Have they been close the entire time? One chickadee flits near, almost landing on my offered palm, and then the piercing eyes and etched feathers dissolve back into twigs and bark. A raven croaks somewhere out of sight. I'm growing cold, growing colder, waiting and hoping for more.

⁕ ⁕ ⁕

Oct. 5. A sideways wind whistles the maple's yellows, oranges, and blended shades. Making no effort to dodge these flying colors, I hike hard, straight through, leaves catching against my body, hanging for a moment before ripping away. At times I enjoy the funny notion that I am a tree and this shedding is proper to me, an ageless ceremony by which I prepare myself for oncoming winter. At other times I go notionless, lost in that droning daze of the trail.

Step-step.

Breath-breath.

Shuffle-shuffle-shuffle.

I've stepped from shallow brown into an ankle-deep pool of magenta. As with the grouse, I'm jolted, though now it's more like waking *into* a dream. The wind cuts out and I pause, tilt back, eye the canopy. A leaf grows, magenta filling my vision. That pigment brushes my cheek, holding there for an instant. I shed it with a smile, good tree that I am.

⁂

Oct. 8. Fat Carl grills me a steak on the fire pit. Barry pours me Polish blackberry brandy. Evil Pete adjusts the volume on some portable speakers piping out an incessant stream of crappy classic rock. Schmitty chops more wood. Randy sits snuggled up in the lean-to, overseeing the action. He's shouting dirty words, dirty jokes, dirty stories. He's speaking with sweeps and jabs of his shaky hands.

What the…?

Hiking after dark, feeling creeped out, picturing the shelter ahead of me as cobwebbed with an eerie loneliness, I resolved myself to an unavoidable encounter with poltergeists. Then I rounded a knob and saw the cheery fire, the propane lanterns. Then I picked up the corny guitar riff, the wailing synth solo, the chaos of snares and cymbals. Then the Randy.

What the...?

This is Connecticut Guy's Weekend, a twenty-some-odd-year tradition, and tonight I'm joining the boys—mostly geriatric engineers and businessmen—for a burst of backcountry fun. It would be easy to judge this sloppy scene as unwanted: normal, noisy, technological life encroaching on the trail's simple, subtle, sacred calm. It would be easy to label it a perversion of wilderness, a disgrace to the midnight woods. But here we are. Here is kielbasa to follow up my steak, and here is pumpkin cheesecake and more brandy to wash it all down. Here is nature, and the humans that are a part of nature.

So sit back, brother, and accept the company. Pray for a decent song. Recline into a full-bellied trance of laugher and hooting owls. Cadge another beer off the Randy, that foul-mouthed, shaky-handed maestro.

⁂ ⁂ ⁂

Oct. 11. It's the fifth caterpillar—specifically, a hickory tussock moth caterpillar—of the afternoon, and she's just like the others: white with black dots and black spikes of hair, incredibly slow. She's working her way across the trail, through gateways of curled leaves, along the rounded edges of crisscrossed sticks. I crouch to better appreciate the effort fueling her tiny journey and soon, through the miracle of sustained focus, through what the poet John Keats described as "a loss of self and a loss of rationality by trusting in the capacity to re-create oneself in another character," our fates merge. No, go left... not *over* that leaf! The leaf tips under our weight, flipping us back to the ground. So be it. We get up and keep going, unperturbed, incredibly slow.

⁂

Oct. 14. Killington Peak is socked in and my sweat is cooling quick. There's no view to be had this evening, no summit picnic. I prepare to leave, lacing my boots tight for what will surely be a slippery, sketchy descent—my favorite kind.

But then, in the corner of my eye, like a rose-toned fantasy, sunset ridges swirl out of the gray. The fabric of sky is thinning, coming apart, fifty miles of countryside appearing through morphing gaps. Swirl. Swoon. Gusting alpine air rushes my eyes, making me cry. I blink off the tears and the clouds swirl back in on themselves, knitting together. The view is gone. Did it exist? Ah, so sweet and frustrating, this world of shifting frames.

⁂

Oct. 17. He's probably eighty years old, hiking solo. Says his name is Dean. Says he spent yesterday contemplating a mirror-smooth pond. "Too great to pass up," he says. "I didn't hike a mile. What's the hurry, anyway?" A slight man, angular, with a towering pack. Pointy beard. Sly grin. "I'm out here for the experiences," he says. "They're all I've ever wanted."

We part—he north, me south—and then the realization hits: Dean is my hero. This man is Vermont's answer to the Chinese mountain sage, the cheery hermit who feasts on dew and flower petals, who sleeps beneath a roof of pinprick constellations. *This* man. *This* openness. What I would give to sit by a pond, just sit by a pond, easy with its reflections, with its ripples, with myself.

Some ways along the trail another realization hits: I can.

⁂

Oct. 20. Intent on finishing the hike, the length, the glory-boredom, the blister-bliss, and hitching a ride home, I pull myself into motion at dawn, gulping the swift creek for coffee, chewing the first climb for breakfast. It's raining, or maybe the rain has stopped and the trees are dripping—I can't tell. I'm looking out from the hollow of my hood, down at the ground, always down at this same-but-different ground. I'm looking, but not really *looking.* A kind of blindness. A kind of stupor. After this many miles, my boots have guidebooks of their own and know exactly how to lead.

Dap-dap-dap. This must be rain, steady on my hood. Or is it? The sound shifts, gets lighter, whispery. It's an infinitesimal shift, audible only to somebody who has been out in the woods for weeks, whose listening has been tuned to smallness by a million small sounds. *Whisk-whisk-whisk. Whish-whish-whish. Whoosh-whoosh-whoosh.* Before sight can register what's happening beyond the protection of my raincoat, hearing makes its pronouncement.

This is no rain. This is snow!

Up into a white forest, a storm of loose wet flakes—I hike for hours, for miles. It's my last day on the trail. It's the end of the line. It's the first snow of the year.

❖ ❖ ❖

There, there, there, there, there: my personal Long Trail, the Long Trail that rose through the soles of my boots, through my legs, through my heart and lungs, and caught as a lump in my throat. It's an unruly mess, but what else could it be? An animal 273 miles long is made of many parts, some social, some ecological, some spiritual, some mundane. What holds the parts together, what flowing blood and electric current unifies them, is something we will never understand.

Sitting at my desk, staring hard at these blank walls, this blank ceiling and floor, I travel again the sprawling body of land. I hike from memory to memory, camping at some, stopping for a snack at others. I dunk a tin cup into one memory. I lean into the fluted song of a second. At the ledge of a third I drop my pack and gaze across valleys of red barns and faded meadows. The Green Mountains are almost leafless, turning purple—ashy—beneath an empty sky.

Autumn is behind me. Canada is very far away. A puddle nearby, papered over, says nothing.

THE HITCH

It was a December morning of strong sun and shining snow, the kind of keen, brilliant, dry-cold morning that tempts some of us to quit our jobs, abandon our possessions, and trot unencumbered into the world beyond routine. I wasn't completely unencumbered myself, but I was going light, and definitely feeling my freedom as I approached the mailbox at the driveway's end and pushed on past. In a lumpy pack I carried the bare essentials for winter camping, along with five ham sandwiches and an ounce of pipe tobacco— my "recreational vagabonding survival kit." My hands were mittened, thumbs toasty on this, their special day.

A quarter mile brought me to the edge of that loud, rushing river known by my fellow Vermonters as Route 7. I dipped a toe in, pulled it out, dipped it in again. Here was a road connected to other roads connected to other roads—the beginning of a new adventure. And here in this first road, mashed against the double yellow, was a wrecked life that was not a life but its opposite: torn black fur, red glistening guts, a hump of meat frozen to the pavement, mangled beyond recognition. I considered approaching the sorry carcass, kneeling, inspecting, maybe mouthing a little prayer, but a truck loomed and I stumbled back. That's when it hit me, gut-punched me, where I was and what I was doing.

So this is what happens when a tender-bodied, warm-blooded, well-meaning creature dares engage, on foot, the violent road-river's relentless flow. In an instant all that makes hitchhiking taboo, its shadow and grit, crowded the front of my mind: psycho killers behind the wheel, tires bearing down in the darkness, loneliness, boredom, icy ditch campsites thick with trash and thorns and skeletons. I raised my thumb like a white flag of peace, offering it to the highway. How good an idea *was* this good idea of mine?

It turned out to be just about the best idea I've ever had, though I wouldn't begin to sense this until twenty minutes later, when my first ride pulled over. The driver's name was Bram and his bumper sticker read, "I Love My Doula." He was clean-shaven, and so was I, having sheared my beard on the hunch that a fresh, friendly face with nothing to hide would increase my appeal as a traveling companion.

"Where to?" Bram asked, a basic question that was difficult to answer given my complete lack of a willful destination. I replied that the goal was to tour our state, letting each ride lead me to the next in a random, aimless chain reaction powered by human generosity and kindness. Bram said he was going to Cornwall, west of Middlebury, and I said fine, onward. Other than a desire to tag the Massachusetts border, and then the Canadian border, and then circle back home—arbitrary goals, a nudge from me to myself in the direction of serendipity—I would impose no design on my travels. Meeting neighbors, slamming pots of drip coffee at general stores, mooing at cows, generally experiencing the villages and vistas and moods that compact-but-huge Vermont has to offer: this was my project.

Bram nodded in understanding. It turned out that he, like many of the fifty-one strangers I cruised with over the course of five days and thirty-six rides, had done some hitching himself. As eighteen-year-olds, he and a friend thumbed from Burlington to Seattle. Crossing the Mississippi River, talking of Huck and Jim and rafts, they hatched a plan to paddle it the following summer. When the time came, though, the friend backed out, and Bram set off solo on the fifty-six-day voyage. More recently, with his seventy-eight-year-old mother in the bow, he canoed the Connecticut River from its headwaters to the Atlantic. The float was Mom's idea.

At a rural intersection north of Cornwall, Bram answered a call on his cell: "I can't speak right now. I'm wrapping up an interesting discussion with a hitchhiker." Our talk had meandered from business ethics, to 401ks, to following passion's idiosyncratic path, to the complicated glee of getting caught in the rain, to living with uncertainty, and now to goodbye. I couldn't thank him enough for the ride, not so much for the miles as for the immensely positive tone it lent the beginning of my trip. Momentum and positive energy were on my side, and I knew right then the very truth that would be proved to me repeatedly in the days to come.

That truth? Hitching is a free ticket to vivid encounters with Vermonters from diverse walks of life, each the embodiment of a story, a personal brand of wisdom, a unique relationship to some feature—a pumpkin patch or antique store—of the shared ground. These stories pass us by every day, in every vehicle we honk at or simply ignore. By providing a time and space for fellow travelers to meet and talk, hitching can slow the stories and, on occasion, invite *them* to invite *us* inside.

Bram and I got out of the car, shook hands, and stood blinking in the sun. Then I was alone on Route 30, white flag in the air.

⸭ ⸭ ⸭

There was more than a lot to take in that first day, and not just the astonishing friendliness of my chauffeur-strangers. Michael, the guitar teacher blasting opera. DeMar, who'd lived his whole life in Idaho and Utah. Xtian, an artsy hipster feasting on a massive block of cheddar cheese, flakes of which somehow kept leaping into my lap. There was landscape, too, so easily forgotten in the rush of a sixty-mile-per-hour conversation, but still elementally present when a ride abruptly ended and I was birthed, warm and confused as a newborn, from the womb of an SUV.

This was perhaps most interesting of all to me, this interplay of riding and waiting, of *automotive* awareness and *pedestrian* awareness. One minute I'd be kicking pebbles to the tune of a distant chainsaw and a pileated woodpecker's percussive lunch. A crooked silo would rise before me, grow larger with each step, and sink beneath the horizon at my back. Small sounds. Small shifts in perspective. Then a car would stop—always, it seemed, when my senses had finally gotten back into my body, my attention back into the land—and off we'd zoom, only to repeat the sequence ten or thirty miles hence. It felt like a constant tug between slow motion and fast-forward, and it left me exhausted at the end of the day.

In classic nearing-the-winter-solstice fashion, that "end of the day" arrived around three. I was riding with Kate, a senior at Green Mountain College in nearby Poultney who dressed in a style that blended elements of hippie, punk, and goth. Kate's rear doors were jammed and didn't open, so my pack was in my lap. Behind us, bedded among clothes and books and candy wrappers, a mop of a dog slept the deep sleep of the camouflaged.

I'd assumed that few, if any, women would pick me up, but in the course of my tour I was actually picked up by six lone women, and twice by a pair of women, so Kate was no exception. She deposited me at the general store in Wells, which had just closed, saying that if I needed a place to warm up, or a hot beverage, I could visit her friends a mile south of town in a teal farmhouse. After talking with a bicycling teenager for a while—he said of my project, "I'm glad you're doing this," and I replied, "I'm glad you're glad"—I strolled to the teal farmhouse, petted the goats outside, then went in and asked permission to camp atop yonder hilly meadow.

Go for it.

Thanks.

And come by for tea tomorrow.

Cool.

Enjoy it.

I will.

That night it snowed and the moon was full and Canada geese rustled the quiet sky with their wings. Dinner was delicious—a ham sandwich and a smoke.

⁂

Try and picture this happening all over again. And then again. And then again. But picture it much wilder than I've described it, not dangerous or threatening or even the slightest bit tense, just weirder, more varied, more exciting and fun.

Picture hunters moving rifles off the passenger seat to make room for me, or mothers moving children, or squinty dudes moving bags of skunky marijuana. Picture me outside the J. Crew outlet in Manchester talking dirt bikes with Randy, or searching back roads for a fish hatchery in Pownal with a New Yorker whose glasses made him resemble a fish. Picture young shaggy carpenters, ski resort snowmakers, cleaning women and their vacuums, a guy who'd never been to Quebec because of his seven felonies, a woman from Wisconsin with a hearing-impaired son and a husband designing yachts in Dubai.

Picture Beth walking her dogs at sunset, instructing me to wait for her at the car: "It's the one with the sticker that says, 'God is my copilot.'" Picture her taking me to her house, feeding me, offering me the barn floor as a bedroom and, in the morning, praying for me, both her hands on my shoulders, the two of us standing in the middle of Route 100 down by the Massachusetts line, our heads bowed beneath a new clear day.

Picture Route 100 itself—so sinuous, so deep in the hollows, so damaged by recent floods. A hurricane came through Vermont three months prior to my hitching trip, came through hard, came through fast and fierce. I rode with a hydrologist named Eli up seventy-five miles of rubble-strewn river valley, each mile a lecture on why this slope eroded, why an excavator shouldn't be in that gully, what these golf course fairways looked like *before* they were littered with tree trunks.

And the towns: Jamaica, Ludlow, Pittsfield, Warren. And

the faces: Laurie, Frank, Rudy and Julie, Brent and snotty toddler Cody. The lady with the dark hairs on her chin who dumped me at McDonalds in Enosburg Falls during a squall. The fir-perfumed logger, his black coveralls coated in fresh yellow sawdust.

I went all the way to Richmond in thirteen rides, the next day all the way to Canada and back to Burlington in ten. I rode in the slushy bed of a pickup missing its tailgate. I unloaded nasty mangled steel at the Swanton scrapyard. I helped change a tire. I heard life plans. I shared a few of my own. I walked for hours—no traffic, no luck, just me and a great blue heron tracing the rim of a pewter lake, flat as the sky. Middle of nowhere? Middle of *here.*

Picture this, and whatever else you can, because whatever you picture is probably out there, bumping along the road right now. Perhaps most challenging of all, picture yourself in a position of weakness, where you need a ride, or warmth, or just a little boost. Picture *choosing* this helplessness, this vulnerability. In the picture you will see a car pulling over and a chauffeur-stranger beckoning you aboard, and then you will understand what I came to understand, what I saw and felt. The goodness of the place and the place's people. The old road-river flow of humanity.

⋄ ⋄ ⋄

My last ride plucked me from noise and exhaust and stunted shrubbery and wind-borne litter, a typical American commercial strip, atypical in Vermont. The driver's name was Jeff. He was heading south to Poultney to spend the weekend drinking whiskey and reminiscing with his cousin, a slate-mining, vineyard-owning Vietnam veteran who, as it turned out, was the landlord of Kate, the hippie-punk-goth I'd met on my first day. We agreed it was a small world, but even as the words came out of my mouth I began to doubt them. Maybe it's a big world, I thought, a massive world, a world so vast and mysterious and interconnected and unpredictable that we are terrified of its potential and must daily shy away from its invitation.

Jeff dropped me a quarter mile from my house—the exact spot where the journey had begun. Route 7 was running quiet and serene. I looked but saw no trace of the animal whose ruined body had filled me with dread five days before, not even a faint bloodstain on the double yellow. To the south, Jeff's truck shrank, the land swelling around it. I stood there in the road for a while, unsure of my next move. It was a warm and melty and pinkish-gray morning, the kind of morning that tempts some of us to quit our jobs, abandon our possessions, and trot unencumbered into the small world, the big world, the world beyond routine.

Hard not to raise a thumb and keep going, I said aloud. My thumb replied with a farewell wave of his flag.

THE SKI

We'd skied nearly three hundred miles of rock, dirt, leaves, moss, ice, crust, apples, slush, logs, lakes, creeks, roads, railways, fairways, snowmobile byways, stubble corn, corn snow, groomed snow, crap snow, coyote-scat-stained snow, and clean white rolling trail. We'd suffered, endured, and enjoyed "the length of Vermont on skis," as *The Catamount Trail Guidebook* puts it. Twenty days. The longest cross-country ski trail in the country. Doing it! Almost *done* with it! And then the Mummy, that obstinate Tutankhamen, just flat-out refused to move.

Stuck. Cuss. Ugh.

Not that this was anything new. A plastic sled weighted with a humanoid, tarp-wrapped, sixty-pound lump of camp gear and supplies doesn't exactly skip and prance from the Massachusetts line to Jay Pass, fourteen trail-miles shy of the Canadian border. That's where we were, climbing through thigh-deep drifts into the fibrillating heart of a two-day blizzard, the first legitimate dump of a weirdly mild winter. Stinging needles of snow flew into our eyes. The wind chiseled at our nostrils. Though I could barely hear it above the raw, whirling din, my hip flexors sang a song of pain and grief. It was miserable, exhausting, utterly real. In a word, perfect.

Cuss-ugh-cuss.

Ross, my partner and tentmate on the journey, and my tromping buddy since preschool days, is a scientific anomaly, a unique hybrid of human and draft animal, and boy was he ever drawing on his mixed genetics during that last push, planting his poles, leaning into the slope, struggling against the harness that tethered him to the recalcitrant Mummy. Ahead, I could make out a flattish area where the trail kinked before steepening—a good place to rest, maybe vomit if I felt plucky. It would be my goal, my destination, my…pink helmet?

The helmet was glossy, like an odd little Barbie spaceship hovering amid the storm. A French Canadian woman with a blond ponytail? She shooshed from the glades and stopped in front of me. A man appeared at her side. They smiled at one another. I figured they were just out for a brief backcountry jaunt, their car parked atop the pass, brimming with cookies and hot cocoa.

"Isn't it a gorgeous day," Pink Helmet said. I nodded, managing something about the next portion of trail, the impending hardship, the vomit. "You have to earn it," she replied, casually, flippantly, as if the phrase held no complicated truth. For emphasis, or perhaps thinking I hadn't heard her over the shrieking gusts and clattering tree branches, she echoed herself: "You have to *earn* it."

Behind me, Ross was on the move, and behind him the track we'd established—the symbol of our effort and achievement—was disappearing beneath blowing white. Cringing at the storm, I sensed all that we had passed through, all the land and weather, ascents and descents, days and nights, and with it the futility of exertion, the absurdity of the universe. Sisyphus came to mind, the poor Greek bastard condemned to push a boulder up a mountain only to have the boulder roll back down to the bottom every time. I envisioned him trading his boulder for a sled, and his mountain for the length of Vermont, and then setting out, with a *cuss* and an *ugh*, not for the first time, not for the last, not exactly dead on his feet, not exactly alive on them either.

My face was accumulating rime. Vomiting now seemed imminent. I blew a snot-rocket directly into my neck warmer, turning toward Pink Helmet, who was smiling at me.

Yeah, I thought. You are so right. You have to earn it. But earn *what*?

‡ ‡ ‡

There are many good reasons to nibble at the Catamount Trail rather than bite the whole thing off in a single, gluttonous expedition, as Ross and I did. Avoiding existential questioning—*Why am I doing this? What is being earned? What happens if my toes freeze and each little piggy dies a cyanotic death?*—is only the tip of the ski pole, as it were. There's also the pleasure of trading the Mummy for a fanny pack, the pleasure of matching an easier or harder section of trail to your taste on a given day, and, most significant, the pleasure of staying at home when the conditions, for lack of a more mature phrase, totally suck.

Which leads to our interest in an immersive, end-to-end ski tour. We wanted to feel, in a very direct, embodied way, everything Vermont winter has to offer, hardships included. Neither of us had ever snow-camped for more than a few nights in a row. Neither of us had ever lived, animal-style, in this famously challenging and rewarding season. You might say that our Catamount Trail expedition was an attempt to come close to the soul of winter, to bring our souls into alignment with this broader, elemental soul, to become cold like the ground, or light like a snowflake, or steady like the track of a moose, or still like the forest beneath the night of spinning stars. Maybe it was communion we were hoping to earn. Maybe this *is* what we earned. Or maybe I'm just rambling and all that happened was a long, grueling ski.

Whatever the motivations, one morning in early February we drove south to Bennington, then over the mountains to Readsboro, where the trail begins. On the way, we cached a box of food at an inn on Route 4, north of Killington, estimating it would take us a week to ski back and retrieve the feast. Noting the brown forest floor of beech leaves and the brown muddy parking lot where the Catamount Trail crossed the road near the inn, I felt a hint of upset. We were at two thousand feet, considerably higher than many portions of the trail, and there wasn't any snow. I preached to myself that expectations could only hurt us—that radical acceptance would be the name of our encounter with the land—but it made no difference. My feet were scared of hiking three hundred miles in stiff plastic Nordic boots, and I was scared for them.

To our relief, the southern section of the state had a base of about four inches: icy, bulletproof, hooray! Those first days were warm, up in the fifties, and the snow kept melting and refreezing into a glaring sheet whose lexicon did not include the word "traction." Your typical day-trip skier would have turned around in disgust. We, on the other hand, felt blessed. Furthermore, we felt blessed when we were fording a bridgeless creek and a steppingstone appeared at just the right distance. And we felt blessed on each short, skiable section of downhill—the alternative, if it was too steep or the severity of a potential crash was too high, being to shoulder the skis and walk. We even felt blessed to find the perfect type of moss to use in lieu of toilet paper. Lowering your standards is not a praised and cherished practice in our culture, but let me tell you, it's empowering. The virtue of contentment. I highly recommend it.

That initial eight-day push passed in a dreamy blur. The alarm would buzz at 5:20 A.M. and we'd boil up a thermos of spruce tea (made from the tree's needles) and a pot of oat-butter soup (made from the pounds of butter that comprised the Mummy's left foot). Pulling on pungent long johns was never easy, nor was breaking camp, but those chores passed, as did the first climb of the day, and the second, and the third. As did a frozen reservoir on the left, a frozen cataract on the right, a conversation, a quiet observation, an abandoned ski resort, a logging operation, a condominium complex, a glacial erratic.

Vermont—a dreamy blur indeed. The skis slid, stuck, edged, floated, broke. We hitchhiked into a village to get my binding fixed. A bald eagle released a spray of whitewash across blue sky. A family of chefs fed us a six-dish Cuban dinner. Friends and acquaintances. Hemlock and black cherry. Bobcat, ermine, kinglet, sparrow. We paused beside a beaver pond in remote woods, because I'd toppled over despite skiing on flat ground, and Ross pointed to scratches on a pine's corrugated trunk. "Bear," he said. "Climbed it last spring."

Each morning the sun showered us through the weave of leafless branches. Each afternoon we devoured sharp cheddar cheese, summer sausage, wadded tortillas. Each evening a bonfire dried our socks, mesmerized us with its glowing, crumbling architecture. And the greatest blessing of them all, the dreamiest of dreamy blurs, found us every night: deepest sleep.

The second week of our trip, the middle chunk of the state, was like the first—but completely different. Things got easier. The existing snow softened. Once or twice a millimeter of fresh snow fell (standards, remember?). Having traveled 150 miles, we finally saw our first skier and first snowmobiler. We met an eighty-nine-year-old man near a mushy spread called Lefferts Pond. "Last year I snowshoed 103 days," he said. "This year, maybe six." We strolled with him for an hour on a gravelly path, skis in our arms, asking questions, listening, absorbing his wisdom and zest. How can such an old man be so fit, so happy, so sharp, so centered? He told us that he'd never stopped "getting out," that it was a priority, that it has to be.

The third week? Oh, you can imagine it. Or maybe you can't. It's just Vermont out there, just the endless marvel of one corner of our endless earth. And the Catamount Trail? Just a crooked line through mountains and fields.

       ⁂

Darkness. The blizzard was still twitching, my hip flexors still groaning and moaning and wailing their pain. We were at the wide, clear-cut swath that marks the end of the United States and the end of the trail, Jay Pass and Pink Helmet distant memories of morning. I tried to take some photos, but my numb trigger finger proved useless. The universe was the bubble of light coming from my headlamp—a universe torn by snow—and it was absolutely absurd.

So what happened, what changed, what was earned? Something, that's for sure, but something hard to name.

Put it this way: I phoned Ross the day after we got off the trail. He was up at Stowe with his girlfriend, out for an afternoon of cross-country skiing. Less than twelve hours prior we'd skied for twelve straight hours, and before that we'd skied for three consecutive weeks. Three hundred miles. The length of Vermont on skis. I hung up, picturing Sisyphus and that eighty-nine-year-old man, picturing Ross on the Stowe trails, maybe even back on a section of the Catamount Trail, gliding free and easy, unencumbered by a Mummy, but otherwise the same.

Insane, I thought. You go and go and go, and all you earn is the desire to go more, which is not desire but love, an abiding love of getting out, of going, of grabbing your boulder, pushing hard, chasing it back down the hill to start anew in the home that holds your life. I reminded myself that Ross is a freak, a mule-man, a genetic weirdo—if he had his way, he'd probably ski straight on through to Labrador.

No thanks, not me. Ice skates in my knapsack, I made for the local creek, predicting good ice. Sitting around on the couch was not an option.

THE BIKE

I offered my name, but he did not reciprocate. I asked if this was private land or a National Forest campground, then stood there in my padded spandex bike shorts, cold and tired and increasingly nervous, waiting for an answer. I asked again. He stared. It was a blank stare—not mean or malicious, just blank. The kind of stare a cinder block would give you if a cinder block had eyeballs. And if a cinder block were drunk.

How could I know that he was drunk? I'd come off one of the big mountain passes and landed at a pond, all silvery and smooth. It was only the first night of my trip, so I didn't need a bath, but I did need a pair of trees to string up my hammock. A bonfire on the far side of the pond grabbed me with its rowdy light. A little yappy-dog, equally rowdy, accosted my ankles. A stack of cargo pallets waited beside the stack already burning. Cigarette behind the ear. Rolling Rock tallboy. The man stared at the flames, or into them, and then at and into me.

After longer than I felt comfortable with—ten seconds, ten minutes, I'm not sure—my host said that he owned this land and, "no doubt," I could camp here if I liked. His voice had barbed wire in it. Cinder blocks, too. He was maybe sixty years old. Wore big boots. A handsome guy if you saw past the missing teeth.

Whatever I was getting myself into wouldn't be easy to get out of, should it come to that, yet the pond was striking, the pallets crackly and warm, and I was intrigued. My goal on this tour was to encounter Vermont, not its Essence or Immutable Being or any such nonsense, but its particulars, those people and places and certain slants of light and shapes of shadow that, when bundled together in consciousness, become the tidy thing I term "home." If this man was Vermont, or some part of Vermont, engage him I must.

I thanked Toothless Host for the invitation—he said, "No doubt, no doubt, no doubt"—and parked my bike, rigged my hammock, returned to the fire with a dinner sandwich. The yappy-dog reared, pawing at my leg, begging, yapping and yapping and yapping. I didn't care, but T.H. got pissed.

The issue wasn't so much *that* he yelled as *how*. It was like a chant, like he was entrancing himself to the rhythms of his own anger. *Beggar, beggar, beggar. Bad, bad, bad.* It was like he'd dropped to the bottom of some deep black well and was trying to climb out, one word at a time, each word a ladder's rung. *Git, git, git.* I asked some question, something about the pallets, and he rose from the depths for a minute only to fall back to the bottom. *Beggar, beggar, beggar.* Hoping to shut the dog up, I scarfed the sandwich fast as I could—but I couldn't scarf fast enough, and Toothless kept on.

A firefly blipped past, looking somewhat like a plane. It made me feel how far away I was, here in these darkening mountains of a Vermont I'd hardly known.

The yappy-dog yapped louder.

Bad, bad, bad.

⁂

In early June, over the course of a week, I rode approximately five hundred miles on a bicycle. This was a new enterprise for me. Before the trip, I'd never pedaled more than thirty or forty miles in a day. A handful of years had seen me on a bike a handful of times.

The route I traveled was designed en route, seat-of-the-spandex-pants-style. I wended from Ferrisburgh to the dirt roads of West Halifax, Green River, and Guilford, then wiggled the east-central side of the state, through Woodstock and South Royalton and Hardwick, plus quieter spots I'd never heard of like Simpsonville and Downers. (I bypassed Goose Green and have not forgiven myself.) Once my initial supply of sandwiches ran out, I found fuel in various combinations of couscous, instant Folgers, granola, powdered milk, and hot water from gas stations. I bought one donut. I slept on a floor, on a porch, in a lean-to, in the anonymous woods. I hit Canada at Derby Line, coasted a gravel path along the edge of Lake Memphremagog, and cranked south, against driving rain, to my sister's in Richmond.

By the time I reached Ferrisburgh on the seventh day, my body was beat up and broke down and other things as well. Back and neck ached. Right knee clicked with the regularity of a metronome. I had that deep bone-bruise sensation in my hands and through my keel. And my legs—if they could rightly be called "legs"—felt weak and trembly, like they might accordion out from under me if I used them for anything but pedaling.

More impressive than the body, though, was the mind, the bent, twisted, scrap heap of a mind that I lived in and with for much of the outing (I'm thinking here of phrases such as "mind *bender*," "sick and *twisted*," "Let's throw some more junk on that *scrap heap*"). A friend who loves bike touring informed me pretrip that I'd probably want Chamois Butt'r for chafing and a set of Allen wrenches for tuneups and that I should expect a variety of complications, mechanical glitches, nagging pains. He even lent me the panniers that his mother used on a tour of Europe in the '70s. It was only my headspace—what would happen to it after consecutive ninety-mile days on the road—that he neglected to mention.

The afternoon I arrived home, after promptly devouring a pound of bacon (straight, no chaser), I traced my route on a road map with a blue marker: sixty-three village-cities, thirty-three creek-rivers, twenty-six lake-pond-reservoirs, ten counties. Keeping track of roadkill proved difficult, so instead I counted types: woodchuck, chipmunk, raccoon, garter snake, red-spotted purple admiral butterflies. Estimating the number of shirtless, pot-bellied men mowing lawns also presented challenges. Weed-whacking included? Is a farmer mowing a hayfield a totally different category?

I taped the map to the wall beside my desk and wrote my stats in the corner. It wasn't enough. I scribbled notes along the route, with arrows pointing to precise locations: *fish-delivery truck, dusty creemee stand, indigo bunting, mondo vista, huffing exhaust!* It still wasn't enough, so I added more: *vile egg water, overpriced sunscreen, snapping turtle, Lower Podunk Road, quiet and undisturbed.* I could see that I'd made my way through rich towns and poor, soaked in streams, befriended a wonderful retired lady who offered me a cabin to live in for the summer. I could *think* Vermont's massiveness and irreducibility, but I couldn't *hurt* with it. Not like when I was out there. Not as a mental scrap heap. Vermont the Particular was already transforming back into Vermont the Bundle, that comforting, easy myth.

⁂

A bicycle covers massive distances quickly—much as a car does—but on a bicycle you are out in the open, senses pricked. This is perhaps obvious. It's the *implications* of this observation that I find fascinating, and that my friend neglected to mention. One cyclist I met near Lake Willoughby, an endurance nut who has traversed the entire country and routinely blasts off 175 miles in a day, referred to car travel as "being in the cage." When biking, you are decidedly free of the cage. Everything from ants on the highway shoulder to thunderheads building in the distance, from the smell of lupine to the smell of diesel, from Brattleboro to Barton—it comes as a deluge, an inundation.

The result? Nausea. Scrap heap. A kind of trippy, overwhelming, kaleidoscopic experience. Barefoot tweaking addict on the public library steps? Gentle hunchbacked grandpa arranging garden gnomes in mulch nests? Child on a tire swing with a smartphone in hand? Snapping turtle? Indigo bunting? Are these folks really neighbors? Am *I* their neighbor? Or am I just a tourist, some fool who should get a paying job, settle in one town, stop rambling and observing and forcing myself to "take it all in"?

Bike touring is not a means to answering these questions. Bike touring is disturbing. And it is awesome *because* it is disturbing. Bike touring is too much: too many beautiful images and too many sad images and too many roads winding toward too many unexpected reversals.

⁑ ⁑ ⁑

When I finished my sandwich, the yappy-dog quieted and jumped into Toothless Host's lap. T.H. was still drunk as a cinder block, but now, instantly, he was tender, petting the dog with the hand not holding his Rolling Rock. We began to talk, and though the conversation veered into incoherence and abrupt pauses and repetition—"no doubt, no doubt"—it *was* a conversation. And not just any conversation, but a good one, a conversation with a man from one of the million Vermonts I've hardly known.

We talked for an hour, talked about many things. How long it takes to burn twenty pallets. How you can heat your house through the winter on lumber-mill tailings. How nice the pond and mountains are in any season. How his ninety-eight-year-old dad and eighty-seven-year-old mom still live in a rickety house back near the pass road. How it wasn't that challenging to establish "perimeters" in Grenada during "that scuffle."

"You know, I was in the service five years," he said, "and there was only one guy I stayed in contact with afterwards, a good Irishman, a good Irishman, my one friend from all that time, and you know, you know what?"

The fire popped, hissed, hushed.

"He blew his brains out."

The stars were sparking, both in the sky and reflected on

the surface of the pond. I said nothing, then something genuine—from the heart—but completely trite.

"It traumatized me," Toothless Host went on. "No, not traumatized, but made me sad, yeah, it made me sad. And it still does. It makes me sad to talk about it."

The dog in his lap snuggled deeper. The night was cold enough to see your breath. No beer left. The last pallet's embers glowing their way to soot.

"It makes me sad to talk about it. No doubt, no doubt. Even right now."

$$\text{\small :\ :\ :}$$

One minute you're climbing a hill, the heat and fatigue and metronomic knee joint conspiring to take you out, finish you for good. The next you're racing three or six or nine miles of smooth new blacktop, your body dissolved in cool wind and wide views. It's a hilly state, a nothing-but-hills state, and on a bicycle you can't help but go up and down, up and down. The transitions between the two—between the up and the down—are nearly imperceptible. They happen in a weary flash. This may be the metaphor I'm wanting.

Or maybe this: one minute you're scared of a man, hyperaware of your differences, your sobriety and his deep black well, your fixed-up teeth and his gaps and spaces, and the next you're inclined to put your arm around him, tell him something heartfelt that isn't trite, or just let him know that you appreciate the invite to camp on his land, that you'll be sure to stop in and say hello the next time you're passing by, that you'd like to meet his folks if that's cool, that the pond and mountains are nice, very fine, such an amazing setting for a bonfire. He says "no doubt," says it again, and swerves homeward, leaving you alone with the bullfrogs and peepers, those last glowing embers.

The moon is rising, the hammock swaying. The knots holding together Vermont the Bundle are loosening. Fireflies aren't planes, they're shooting stars. And this—this is only the first night of the trip.

THE PADDLE

It was Friday night and my dad, whom I hadn't seen since we'd come off the Connecticut River a week earlier, was in a cheeky mood. All twinkle-eyed, he kept saying, "I don't want to influence what you write about our trip, but you might throw in phrases like 'handsome bowman,' 'dedicated sixty-one-year-old father,' or even something simple as 'excellent paddle buddy.'" I told him I appreciated that phrase—*paddle buddy*—but that my inclination was to focus more on the river than on us.

"If I were to write about you," I said, "it'd probably be in the service of describing the river, the subtle ways it works over dinky little humans." He nodded. A week at his office, swimming upstream against emails, meetings, assignments, and stress, had undoubtedly taken its toll. But the memory of our time on the real thing was still fresh. We'd partaken in the flow. The silt was under our fingernails.

"Which is just to say," I went on, "that I'd probably write about the time I thought you'd died."

Another nod. "You mean when we flipped and the canoe shot into the air and I got sucked up by the whitewater and disappeared."

In the approximately 260 miles of river that we explored between the small town of Canaan and the small town of Vernon—miles rich with bald eagles, largemouth bass, slapping beaver tails, oxbows, covered bridges, party barges, cornfields, submerged tires, protruding logs, lily pads, and dawdling clouds—there was only one rapid where a paddler could actually flip his craft and disappear beneath a flexing muscle of water. I remembered swimming out of that flex, turning to confirm that Paddle Buddy was following, and seeing only his hat floating after me. For all I knew, the river had him in a headlock.

"No, not that time," I said. "The *other* time I thought you'd died."

⁂

Day four. Early afternoon. Sky like a gray ceiling. We weren't in Ryegate, Vermont, *or* Bath, New Hampshire. Rather, we were *between* the two, me in the stern, Dad in the bow, both of us dipping, pulling, and redipping our paddles to the same unheard but deeply felt beat.

Here was the hub of a 7.2-million-acre watershed, and here, too, was a feeling of bioregional centeredness. As Gary Snyder says in an essay on sense of place: "Nature, which is actual, is almost a shadow world now, and the insubstantial world of political jurisdictions and rarefied economies is what passes for reality." Technically, New Hampshire owns the river all the way over to the Vermont shore. Good luck telling that to the birds and fish and long-distance canoeists.

Five hundred feet wide, fringed with patches of marsh, walled with steep wooded banks: the river was actual all right. There were no cottages on the shore, no other boats on the water. A heron prowled the shallows off the starboard side. A kingfisher rattled calls from a twiggy perch to port. Our map showed a dam five miles downstream at Dodge Falls—the seventh of twelve that we would portage around over the course of a week. Some dams were breached, their broken concrete blocks overgrown with wildflowers. Others were close to two hundred feet tall, gloomy and noisy, cranking out power. Many backed the river up into a black, unmoving lake. The dam at Dodge Falls was, apparently, one of these.

An eastern kingbird curled after insects in buoyant, acrobatic sallies, highlighting, by contrast, my midday, flat-water fatigue. Dad must have felt the same because, without saying anything or even glancing at me, he stowed his paddle and lay back, resting his head on one of the rubber dry bags tucked behind his seat. It was a comfortable boat-bed, almost like a cradle, and the first time I'd seen him use it. He lay with his eyes shut, face to the sky. Fifteen minutes later, realizing that he hadn't shifted or made a single noise, I began to wonder. The cradle somewhat resembled a coffin.

I jerked the canoe with a few deliberately crappy strokes. Nothing.

There were two potential explanations. The first was our daily routine. Every morning at seven, I'd wake, boil coffee on a stove in the tent vestibule, scratch my bug-bitten, ivy-poisoned ankles, and read from Thoreau's *A Week on the Concord and Merrimack Rivers*. Though written in the 1840s, and on a different waterway, Thoreau's observations hold true for the contemporary Connecticut. He describes fishermen in their skiffs floating through the reflections of trees, birds darting through the reflections of trees, trees leaning to touch the reflections of trees, and the perceptual challenges of looking *through* the reflections of trees to the pebbly or muddy or weedy river bottom below. In a burst of early American ecoterrorist rhetoric, Ol' Henry even endorses taking a crowbar to the dam at Billerica, Massachusetts, in the name of free shad. *Free Shad! Viva the Actual!* Along with instant coffee sludge, these passages got me psyched for ten hours at the helm.

Ten hours. That's about how long we paddled each day, sometimes with the help of a rippling current, sometimes with the help of a lesser current, the kind noticed not in the body but in the motion of goose feathers and pollen swirls on the river's elastic surface. As I've mentioned, there were long, straight, monotonous stretches as well. And there was tedium, a dull pain in the shoulders.

Don't get me wrong—it wasn't moving sofas or chopping wood or anything. In a canoe you're sitting. You're taking breaks to swim, snack on peanuts, cast the fishing pole (that is, until you lose it in the whitewater). When bridge shadows band your bare chest, you slip over to a sandy beach and Dad scrambles up to the road. He's carrying empty water bottles, searching for a gas station where he can fill them so as to avoid the mouse-tinkling-into-a-Nalgene misery of the backpacking pump. Not wanting to risk breaking the spell, the centeredness that has taken hold of your mind and body with its damp, velvet hand, you stick with the river, twiddling your toes.

Time. It passes. It stops. It does whatever it does when a person quits caring what it does. Dad returns with potato chips, chocolate bars, and a Styrofoam container of General Tso's Chicken from some boondock Chinese takeout joint. You recount for him the story of a bad deli sandwich that crippled you with gut pain during the trip's all-night-first-night thunderstorm, but it doesn't seem to register. He's poring over the map, sticky white rice clinging to his beard. And then you're paddling again, paddling again, paddling again.

The river meanders through open farm valleys and pinched misty canyons, past green tractors in green fields and a running red fox. Sliding toward evening—thirty, thirty-five, forty miles—its persistence is intense, its "ancient, ineradicable inclination to the sea," as Thoreau would put it, both mesmerizing and exhausting. There's no backing up. This liquid channel is an arrow pointing one direction, call it Vernon or call it Long Island Sound. If a coffinish cradle should appear on some dreary afternoon, almost anybody—dedicated sixty-one-year-old father or not—would surely accept the offer.

There was something about the way Dad eased from up-rightness to naptime, though, something so calm and deliberate and final about it that I had to consider an alternate explanation. Perhaps, I thought, he'd altogether let go of the "insubstantial world" above the bank. Perhaps he'd become one with the river. Perhaps he was matching its horizontality with his own. It didn't strike me as the least bit tragic. For days the fish had been jumping and the birds diving, everything converging at the same spot on the same blank plane of water where an insect is swallowed, where dry meets wet, light meets dark, life meets death. I could feel it: Dad had *chosen* this. He was retiring with style, embracing his place in the Actual.

A spider legged toward me on the gunwale. My paddle dripped and dove. The dam would appear soon and I'd have to make a decision. Do I go find help, borrow a phone, break the news and the spell of the river? Or do I throw Paddle Buddy over my shoulder, portage him around the dam like Thoreau would a sack of melons and potatoes, and snag the canoe and dry bags on a second trip? The river is such a mellow place, so peaceful and serene. If Paddle Buddy had in fact gone Actual, why not savor a last dusk together? Sadness, mourning, all that could wait. On the other hand, my neck still felt cramped from previous portages, and I doubted that I had the extra labor in me.

The spider transitioned from the gunwale to the glossy varnish of my paddle shaft, moving in the direction of my knuckles. There was so much river left ahead of us, I thought, digging in harder, the canoe lunging forward. So many clover-field campsites and osprey nests. So many quick rains and rope swings. So many crayfish. Every day at five o'clock, Dad had insisted we stop for a swim, and when we got back in the canoe, wet and refreshed, he'd tell me that these dénouement hours were his favorite. The paddling was not a chore but a meditation, the sun not set but setting.

Five o'clock would soon be upon us. The decision was easy. I dug, certain as only a father's son can be that Paddle Buddy would have wanted it this way.

And then, as easily and unassumingly as he'd reclined, Dad sat up. Neither of us said a word. He lifted his paddle, a kingbird sallied, and on we slowly went.

⁙ ⁙ ⁙

Years ago, I had a philosophy professor who argued that ancient Greek psychology was rooted in the idea that "you become like the object you intend," which is just a fancy-pants way of saying that the things we focus on, spend time with, commit our senses to, and think about, somehow manage to sneak inside of us, transforming who and what we are. For example, if you eat beside a river, sleep beside a river, bathe in a river, stare at a river, and live on a river for 150 hours with minimal interruption, you will become like that river. You won't outwardly show it, but you will feel it. You will feel less yourself, or at least less your "regular" self, that character who too often struggles against a current of emails, stress, and rarefied, insubstantial whatever.

So, then, what's it like to become a river? Is it like a delightful version of multiple personality disorder, like becoming a sexy-curvy lady, an old man in a rumpled, smoke-colored suit, a Zen priest, a marathon walker, and a drowsy, yawning child all at once? Is it like the converse, the river's different faces and qualities collapsing inward to form one unified body? Sitting at the helm ten hours a day, musing bioregionally, I recalled that my body is a sculpture of water. I saw my fluid self as just another drop shuttled by the topography into this larger central flow. I saw myself absorbed. It was like death, like losing yourself in something bigger, some ancient, ineradicable inclination.

But that's soggy nonsense. That's a rambling man, silt still fresh beneath his fingernails. Feeling like a river is, in fact, nothing so philosophical or complicated. You stow your paddle, lie back against a dry bag, ease off into reverie. White birds fly low, bending their wings to touch white-winged reflections. A tree looks at itself, kisses a mirror with its leaves. The sky is gray. Everything is soft, rounded, actual, and okay. Even the Chinese food is sitting decent.

You wake up. Or maybe you don't. Maybe you're still snoozing. You feel like a river and you feel like yourself. You grab your paddle—and everything glides.

THE SWIM

Searching the crawl space beneath a friend's New Jersey beach house, I find two foam boogie boards. One is powder blue, the name Wave Princess printed in a curly font. The other is dandelion yellow, thicker by an inch, labeled Mach 7-7. I'm drawn to Wave Princess—she seems a more appealing companion for what's bound to be a long and intimate journey—but I have some doubts about her buoyancy. I try to imagine her as a floating island, a slab of portable terra foama bobbing in the vastness of our nation's sixth-largest lake. I try to imagine towing her with parachute cord, or kicking behind her, or clinging desperately beneath a purple sky ripped ragged with lightning. The images won't come, and instead I see only bubbles—the bubbles that rise to the surface when a young adventurer sinks into the abyss like a living, breathing stone.

The goal is simple and admittedly weird: swim the 120-mile length of Lake Champlain. Has anybody dared attempt this? Has the notion excited others, maybe the name-giver, French explorer Samuel de Champlain, back in 1609? It's been exciting me for years, ever since I heard about Roger Deakin's book *Waterlog*, which recounts how he linked seas, rivers, lakes, canals, and pools into a swimming tour of the British Isles. Deakin was after a fresh perspective, what he called a "frog's-eye view." He sought to rewild his familiar home. This made sense to me and still does.

My fellow Vermonters insist that I'm unhinged, that I'll surely get run over by an inebriated boater or bopped on the dome by a water skier, and that, best-case scenario, I'll end up a freaky, prune-y mess. When not waxing dermatologic, they emphasize the energetic demands the expedition will put on my already skinny body. How will you handle, how will you deal? I don't know what to say. Some questions can't be answered, only explored. I want to engage my inner frog, that's all.

Securing a pepperoni sponsorship from Dakin Farms, a local purveyor of fine pork products, I congratulate myself: *should the expedition founder, at least this one accomplishment will float me to glory!* A friend recently organized a mountain-bike race sponsored by Clif Bar, so I pop by his house, and he loads me up with seventy sample-sized leftovers. I remove the dense brown protein-turds from their wrappers and transfer them to a single Ziploc. Another Ziploc receives couscous, powdered milk, red pepper flakes, and oregano. Three meals a day, three items on the menu.

I stuff the food into a rubber dry bag, then stuff another with sleeping bag, hammock-tent, change of clothes, jack-knife, lighter, map, and a pocket-sized New Testament given to me years ago by a kindly, white-haired evangelist lady during a hitching trip in Colorado. Space is at a premium in the dry bags, and the New T. is my library's thinnest volume. Anyway, a little salvation might not be the worst thing to have on board.

By early August the lake is up to seventy-four degrees, a delightful temperature, though I do worry that ten hours immersed, day after day, will take me for all the pepperoni calories I'm worth. I spend a couple afternoons rounding up gear: wet suit, neoprene socks, sun hat, flippers, snorkel, mask. A concerned mother (in this case not my own) donates a neon-salmon flag on a fiberglass pole. The flag recalls a polyester T-shirt of the exact same horrible shade that's buried like a dirty secret in my dresser drawer. *Good luck running me over now, you drunk-ass boaters!* In my new outfit, I feel more than practical. I feel aqua-chic.

I'm planning to leave on Monday, but prior to *bon voyage* I need to test my ride. Tenderly, tactfully, I break the news to Wave Princess. *You're just too dainty…I promise, baby, I'll write you every day.* Mach 7-7 is a brute, and that's reassuring. I stab the flagpole into his "bow" and lash my dry bags tight with some shabby clothesline, then head to Whiskey Bay at Thompson's Point in Charlotte.

It's sunset time, giddy-beauty time. A hefty woman thrashes madly in the shallows, wrestling herself onto an inflatable pool toy while simultaneously extolling its virtues. "They're the best," she tells me. "They're from a company in Florida. They're not like other floats. Anybody can get on them." The toy is, essentially, a limp plastic quilt. "You should really use one of these on your mission," she says, still thrashing. I tell her I'm confident my boogie will do the trick.

It does. A flop, an eruption of droplets, and I'm tracking steadily toward the middle of the lake, cormorants passing left and right, the reflections of blush clouds breaking and reforming around me. A gull lands nearby, ripples spreading. I discover that I can beach my upper body on the boogie and propel myself with kicking alone, can even rest my cheek on the dry bags as if they're pillows. This kickboard style is relaxing and fast. It leaves a wake. *I* leave a wake. There's no denying the obvious: I'm a frog-man, a man-boat, some peculiar pepperoni-eating *thing* this ancient, colossal, wonderful, welcoming puddle has never seen.

⸸ ⸸ ⸸

"Should I pee in my wet suit now or wait until I'm in the water?" My sister, who's driven me to the Benson Landing boat ramp, the lake's southern reach, pretends to puke. Her dog, Percy, barks at me as if it doesn't much matter. I waddle the slick concrete ramp in my flippers, canine nephew following. The water is warm, weedy, brown as milky coffee. I'd love to christen myself with a shower of champagne, but don't have any. In lieu of bubbly, I release—*ahhh*—and so begins a bizarre trip.

Walking the muddy shore, my sister encourages me with words I can't hear over slaps and splashes. An immature bald eagle soars low circles, pulling my attention just long enough for some monster, some sturgeon or nightmare snake, to brush against my elbow. Adrenaline sets me flapping like a duck, though of course I'm not a duck: I'm a man-boat. "It's fine," I yell to my sister. "Only a floating stick. Nothing to worry about here. Not going to die in the mouth of some unknown-to-science fish." She laughs, and Percy, who is the opposite of man-boat's best friend, turns and swims away.

Within an hour the novelty and nerves (and warming urine) have washed off. The shore is distant, the nearest house farther. A single monarch butterfly skitters through the massive sky. I'm without distraction—from myself, from my task, from the length of lake extending before me. I *feel* that length, and what it feels like is work, labor, unavoidable toil. My legs have clocked in, and my outfit is no longer amusing, my boogie no longer an oddity. Already I'm shrinking down, regaining a sense of scale proper to a human being. No, not regaining, but reclaiming, proudly *choosing* this smallness.

A wind builds up. Waves slosh around my head. My world is the sound of water, a sound outside time.

⁘ ⁘ ⁘

I'd assumed this would be a social trip: slugging beer with beer-slugging fishermen, eating cheeseburgers at family picnics, fielding friendly "what-in-the-hell-are-you-up-to?" inquiries. It turns out that the bulk of my social interactions, including those I have with common mergansers and northern leopard frogs, are slow-motion stare-downs unaccompanied by the faintest nod of recognition.

A fancy couple in a yacht stares at me through binoculars. A woman in a kayak stares with a hand shading her face. And I stare back, just as incredulous. I've successfully rewilded myself, and now what once passed for semi-normal appears strange. Fast, noisy, expensive cigarette boats are as surprising and disconcerting to me as I am to the men—always men—behind their wheels. Jet Skiers blowing donuts at dusk are like alien invaders from a distant planet.

For the most part, though, I don't see many people. Nothing much happens, at least not in the usual way we think of something "happening." An Adirondack cloud becomes, over the course of an hour, a Green Mountain cloud. *This* tern catches a fish on its first plunge, whereas *that* tern needs three tries. I let go of the boogie, swim free, dive deep with open eyes, deep into yellowy-greens, deeper into greeny-blacks. Kicking again, I consider those hues.

Maybe I consider them for twenty minutes, maybe three days. Often I sing nonsense songs and whimsical shanties. Sometimes, my cheek on a dry-bag pillow, I forget that I'm singing and startle myself.

There's generally a moment in the early afternoon when I recognize that I've been in the water for five straight hours, that I'm absolutely exhausted, that the duct tape protecting my blistered toes has come loose, and that I am not only *still* singing, but also hearing grand elegant symphonies in the splishing rhythm of my flippers. Which is to say I'm hallucinating. Which is to say lunchtime.

I haul out on an island or a mudflat or just around the bend from some mansion's mansion-like version of a dock, and promptly undress. This is not exhibitionism. Without a towel, and fearing that if I don't regularly dry off I will rot, my only resort is to bake in the sun, totally nude, while rolling around on hot, blue stones. If I suspect that I'm burning, I spread the map over my paler regions as a sunshade. When I feel deserving, I eat an entire stick of pepperoni, casing and everything, in two minutes flat. The Clif Bars have melted into a gnarly bowling ball of chocolaty sustenance. For dessert, I pry loose a chunk.

I swim until twilight, the lake's intense flatness working me over like a rolling pin, gently but forcefully smoothing my thoughts until there are few thoughts left to smooth. This is the meditation of water, a liquid state of consciousness that delivers me to night. Camped on shingle beaches, my hammock swings from the sculpted, serpentine branches of half-dead cedars. I eat couscous mush, pile pebbles, read scripture until a paragraph repeats, repeats, repeats—and I'm asleep.

Dreaming breaststroke. Dreaming red-eyed loons with cross-hatched plumage. The groan of thunder wakes me, the storm loud and flashing. I slip out of the hammock and raise my empty bottle to the water streaming off the rain-fly's corner. It's a spiritual cliché, but in this instance it's literally true: man-boat drinks from the source. The New T., by comparison, fails to quench thirst.

⁂

Around five o'clock on the tenth day, having spent much of the previous forty-eight hours riding the swells and troughs of a burly south wind, that wind shifts—U-turns—and slaps me in the face. I'm approaching the causeway connecting Alburgh Tongue with Isle La Motte, beyond which, out of sight, the lake's final arm stretches for the Canadian border. Wild air rushing across that unseen arm drives surface water toward a single opening in the causeway. The opening is a tunnel, its mouth the size of a garage door. I fight for it, pass through, and emerge into sun and gleaming chop. The Rouses Point Bridge is a couple miles off. Sprinting straight toward me: 9 billion waves.

No passport. Close enough. Don't need the customs agents harpooning me or whatever.

As I'm dragging myself onto the causeway's slimed rocks and zebra mussels, stripping off my wet suit one last time, something happens in my neural circuitry—an involuntary twitch—and I'm sent whizzing through history, back past the steamboat Ticonderoga, back past Burlington when it was the third-largest port in the world, a mill town for boreal forest timbers en route to Boston. I pick out faces from the crazy blur: Benedict Arnold in a gunboat, Sam Champlain in a canoe. I see a mile-tall ice sheet creeping from the polar cap, depressing the land with its impossible weight.

Pause. Now I'm moving forward, slaloming the centuries. The ice recedes and the Atlantic pours in—carrying whales and walruses—via the Saint Lawrence channel. Caribou and mammoth roam the tundra coast. Hunters take them with spears. The land rebounds and the sea flows out. Sky falls into the basin as rain and snow. Liking the feeling of earth against its skin, it stays on as a lake.

Then it's over, just like that. The vision is over and so is the voyage. I sit atop my boogie: naked, glutted on pepperoni, wrinklier than a ninety-year-old grandpa left too long in the bath. My flag snaps in the wind, a pinpoint of neon-salmon ugliness in the great sweep of time and space. I'm a man-boat and a shipwreck of a man, humble and happy and properly in place. I'm wee as a frog—a northern leopard frog. Wee and dazzled by the view of those 9 billion waves.

THE FLIGHT

A year ago, after living much of a decade in the American West, I drove from the Pacific Ocean's curling aquamarine tubes and slicing dolphins—drove fast, drove nonstop, eyes burning, right leg stiff from keeping on the pedal—to Vermont, my blood-and-bone home. Within forty-eight hours of arriving, I'd hefted my backpack and stepped onto, stepped *into*, the Long Trail. South from the Québec border. Skimming clouds and swirling rainbow leaves. The trip lasted twenty days and ended at the Massachusetts line in a snowstorm, its ending the beginning of something so much bigger.

Sitting alone on a dark bus that snowy night, heading north through the storm, sipping from a canteen the precious last drops of stream water I'd collected in the state's southernmost crease of wilderness, I parsed my experience. I'd seen so much, so many mountain faces, so many turns of trail. I'd gaped at countless vistas, been soaked by rains, dried by sun. I'd slept on the ground and been filled with its dreams of moss and mice, of dirt and schist, of human hikers curled in rest. My brain hurt with the question: how does it all hold together?

That's when the image from Aristotle came to me, the image that defies imagining—an animal one thousand miles long, a sprawling body that can never be seen in its entirety from any single angle. Too big, this body. Unfathomable. And yet real, tangible, an animal whose parts and places we can engage and, in a sense, come to know. The Green Mountain spine. The spine of an immense, living being. I relaxed into my seat, snow-darkness surging past the bus windows, relishing the idea.

Six weeks after the Long Trail, I took a hitchhiking trip. Another six weeks passed and I embarked on a three-week ski tour. It went forward like this: five hundred miles balancing a bicycle, 260 miles wobbling a canoe, ten days

swim-camping Lake Champlain. I wallpapered my basement office with road maps, plotting routes and paths and
tracks on them in blue ink. Between trips, I wandered these
maps, lost in fantasies of future journeys and memories of
journeys past. Each blue thread was an animal one thousand miles long. Vermont appeared before me in that win-
dowless space as a menagerie.

Nearing the end of my traveling year, I allowed myself
a treat I'd been anticipating for months, since the very moment I turned from the Pacific and gassed eastward: I plot-
ted all the routes and paths and tracks onto a single map.
Blue threads—blue stories—ran parallel, crisscrossed,
bunched up, knotted, frayed out. They covered ground, as
I had.

Though my excursions have been characterized by openness and uncertainty, I've known from the outset how this
project would find its end. October would disappear into
the churn of seasons and be spit back up twelve months
later. Geese and leaves would fly, and I would take to the
air with them. I fantasized that after a solid year of exploration I would rise from the folds of land—those folds where
creeks collect and we bend to drink specifics, details, *this*
current, *this* pool—to see Vermont all at once, unified and
whole. Even if it lasted a mere second, I wanted to gather the
threads of my journeys and braid them together.

The impossible view. Everything at once. My best
chance, I figured, was a plane.

⸭ ⸭ ⸭

Frank Gibney—retired army helicopter pilot, retired air force fighter-jet pilot, friend of a friend, nice guy—agreed to meet me at the Shelburne Airport's grass strip at nine in the morning. He was late. Waiting, I chatted with another pilot who flies out of Shelburne. I'd never been up in a small plane before and asked what to expect. "Fast and vast," he said, "fast and vast." The day was cool, sunny, cloudless— perfect for turtlenecks and hundred-mile views.

Frank arrived and we pushed his RV-6—a sleek, snug two-seater that clocks 170 miles per hour—out of its hangar. In the cockpit, among the dials, switches, and gauges crowding the faux-wood control panel, I spied a plaque. Hardly larger than a stick of gum, it read, "Passenger Warning: This aircraft is amateur built and does not comply with federal safety regulation for standard aircraft." Fiddling with his iPad, Frank briefed me on safety. "Should we get on the ground and I'm not conscious and you are," he began, "in that pack behind the seat there's a black, zippered container, and inside that black, zippered container there's a yellow box. You flip the antenna up on that yellow box and it automatically puts out a distress signal. Okay?"

I nodded, but he didn't see, his attention on two rubber bands that "helped" a dangling cord link with the iPad. The iPad contained important flight software. It wasn't working. "Be careful not to knock the rubber bands," Frank said.

After a half hour of miscellaneous preparations, we stepped onto the plane's wings and lowered—or maybe I should say *stuffed*—ourselves into sardine-seats. Frank slid a glass hatch and locked it, bubbling us in. He started the engine. Propeller blades on the nose of the plane blurred and disappeared. Smell of exhaust. Deafening mechanical noise.

Wearing radio headsets that allowed us to communicate despite the roar, Frank sounded like he was a centimeter tall and sitting in my ear. "Do you suffer from air sickness?" I said it had never been a problem in the past, but that my belly couldn't make any promises. Apparently, that was enough reassurance, because without delay we taxied— *bump, bump, bump*—to the end of the green runway.

A minivoice, broken with static, welled up in the headphones. Frank slipped into jargon, the voice replied in kind, and we charged forward. The roar grew louder. And then the sky was everywhere and everywhere and everywhere.

⁂

Mutton Hill. Shelburne Pond. Richmond. Sunset Ridge. Elephant's Head. Trapp Family Lodge. Waterbury Reservoir. Winooski River. Camel's Hump. Appalachian Gap. Lincoln Peak. Breadloaf Wilderness. Brandon Gap. Chittenden Reservoir. Pico. Killington. Rutland. Route 7. Route 30. Mt. Equinox. Bennington Battle Monument. Route 9. Glastenbury Wilderness. Prospect Ski Area. Somerset Reservoir. Searsburg Wind Power Facility. Harriman Reservoir. Vermont Yankee Nuclear Power Plant. Vernon Dam. Brattleboro. Landscape of rounded hills, bedrock whales slumbering beneath ocean-blankets of trees.

We landed in Springfield—one runway, no waiting—for fuel and lunch. The man in the office told us this was the oldest airport in Vermont, that Charles Lindbergh had given a speech here in 1927 to an audience of thirty thousand. A black-and-white photograph hung by the door: crowds in a field, aviator on a stage, lots of flags and bunting. I scanned the scene for cows but saw none. Frank and I borrowed a car, ate at a diner, returned to the plane, and flew away.

Traveling at different altitudes, sometimes "down in the weeds," as Frank put it, and sometimes up at three thousand or four thousand or five thousand feet, I realized that an aerial perspective has a habit of funneling the eye and mind toward bold, familiar features. From Springfield it was all Mt. Ascutney. From Mt. Ascutney it was all Connecticut River. The river led us over Sumner Falls, the bridge at Fairlee, cornfields, oxbows, and north to Moore Dam. From there it was I-91 and St. Johnsbury. From there it was Lake Willoughby.

We shot the gap between Mt. Hor and Mt. Pisgah, our wings awesomely close to nicking vertical cliffs. Things happen quickly at 170 mph—thoughts come and go like beaver ponds, like villages whose names you can't quite place. Two seconds of searching for peregrine falcons had me remembering a favorite quote from J. A. Baker: "The peregrine lives in a pouring-away world of no attachment, a world of wakes and tilting, of sinking planes of land and water." Of course, the quote also poured away, and the cliffs, unattached, tumbled off in our invisible wake. We banked, the horizon tilting and sinking. From there it was the Northeast Kingdom, scratched with crimson swamps, bruised with autumn's yellow-brown. That man at the Shel-burne Airport was right. *Fast and vast.*

At the edge of Nulhegan Basin we pivoted above a log-ging operation and flew due west: Lake Seymour, Derby Center, Lake Memphremagog, the Jay Peak tram. Survey-ing Jay Pass, I remembered my first day on the Long Trail twelve months prior and knew what I wanted to do. The landscape, with a speechless gesture, was telling me.

What I wanted was here-and-there, was micro-to-macro, was *all*, was *this*. What I wanted was another hike, another hitch, another seven or ten or twenty-five or two hundred lengths of Vermont. I wanted to spend the rest of my life flowing with the seasons, across the land like water, across the water like sky. I wanted to ink routes and paths and tracks onto maps until the paper gave out, until office walls were tattooed blue forever. I wanted to crawl the length of the state. I wanted to snowmobile it. I wanted to ride a horse, trim a sail, lace skates, rappel into caves, climb to the canopy, get drunk at a bar, stumble to the next. I wanted to touch this huge-little state with the paws of lynx, the ex-pertise of botanists, the schedule and routine of UPS truck drivers, the hunger of spiders. I wanted to nap in hollow logs and hot-tub at lavish mansions. I wanted to hunt fossils. I wanted to dodge lightning. I wanted to darken my sight and hear. I wanted to close my thinking and feel. I wanted to ramble myself oblivious.

Want, want, want—the view filled me with desire. I wanted to give myself entirely, not for a year but for good, not as a project but as a living and dying, a passing through and beyond. If I'd had a parachute, I swear I would have jumped right then and there, for in that brief moment—a moment that poured away as moments must, a paradoxically unattached and totally attached instant—nothing could have sounded so sweet as to free-fall into the infinite invitation that is the terrain of home.

⁑ ⁑ ⁑

All told, Frank and I spent just under four hours curving and diving and rising, the RV-6 tipping a wing to every major geographic region in the state, including stretches that represented each of my previous adventures. The feeling of the day—like visiting dear friends—put a lump in my throat. There was a mysterious power in the repeated nodding, or bowing, of my head to specific places I'd visited, taken shelter, watched the sun go down and moon come up. These were places that had become more than places. By getting out, traveling, looking, listening, smelling, tasting, and touching, I'd turned them into neighbors, family, brothers and sisters. I know it sounds cheesy, corny, sentimental, but they'd become parts of myself, and I—*who is this guy, this me?*—a part of them.

Barry Lopez has called the land an "animal that contains all other animals." If that's not beautiful, I don't know beauty, don't know anything. The land contains squirrels and ducks and children as it contains animals one thousand miles long. I wanted to see this ultimate animal, if only for a split second. Naturally—*naturally*—I didn't. Instead,

I saw its parts. The wholeness of Vermont, of any stretch of earth, can be understood, maybe even experienced as a tingle in the nerves, a rush in the blood, but it can never be observed. It skips into shadows, elusive and flickering. It hides in the sun's fire, too bright to perceive. The best we can hope for is a glimpse of fin or wing or tail, a gas station or esker or unkempt orchard, a scat or school playground, a shifting drift of snow. But let me be clear: these glimpses are enough.

⸭ ⸭ ⸭

Swanton. Isle La Motte. Malletts Bay. Burlington. Thompson's Point. Little Otter Creek. Mt. Philo. Shelburne's Vermont Teddy Bear Company. U-turn. Hold on tight. *Frank, you wacky sonofa…*

Grass landing strip speckled white with gulls.

Those speckles rose before us and the afternoon's brassy rays exploded off smudges of insect guts on the glass bubble. The wheels touched. The flight was complete. The year, which can never be complete for it is always already morphing into the next, wished me farewell. I thanked Frank for an amazing day and Vermont for an amazing experiment, an amazing immersion. And for my life. And for being an animal to us all.

The propeller blurred into visibility and the roaring noise went mute. We pulled the glass, unbuckled, stretched. Through the exhaust I detected the scent of leaves and wood smoke. In the newfound quiet, I heard honking. Overhead, geese flew south, a tight formation, the animal rolling beneath them, beneath me, rolling and spinning, spinning on its axis, whirling in the cosmos.

I stepped from the wing of the plane to the ground and, though it may be obvious, I'll say it anyway, for certain truths deserve repeating, certain repetitions always welcome: the ground felt solid beneath my feet. Solid and good. Solid and good.

Credits and Acknowledgments

Rather than name a bunch of names, I'll just say that if you are mentioned in this book, please accept my hearty thanks. This goes for all the writers I referenced and directly quoted, and all the people, both strangers and friends, with whom I traveled. Many individuals offered support in various ways but don't appear in the text, and they too deserve my thanks. I'm thinking of small, priceless gifts: rides to the trailhead, meals when I was hungry, floors for sleeping, borrowed equipment, good cheer, on and on.

I should specifically nod my head in gratitude to Dakin Farm and Shelburne Farms, Blueberry Hill Inn and Trapp Family Lodge and Inn at Long Trail, and also to the San Francisco Public Library system and the Old Rock Community Library of Crested Butte, where portions of the book were written.

In large part, my stories exist thanks to various editors who supported their creation: Phil Jordan and Kathleen James at *Vermont Magazine*, Annie Stoltie at *Adirondack Life*, Mel Allen at *Yankee*, Patrick White at *Northern Woodlands*, Pamela Polston at *Seven Days*, Scott Gast at *Orion*, and everyone working behind the scenes at these publications. Of course, the book exists *as a book* thanks to the enthusiasm, effort, and skill of Steffanie Mortis, Tom Payton, Sarah Nawrocki, and the rest of the team at Trinity University Press.

Finally, there's me. I exist—as a reader and writer, as a wandering appreciator (or is that appreciative wanderer?) of the natural world—thanks to my parents, my sister, my grandparents, some aunts and uncles and cousins, a bunch of friends, a handful of teachers, a special lady, and various dogs, birds, mountains, waters, and open fields. As Raffi sings in a nice song of his: "Thanks a lot, thanks for all I've got."

‡ ‡ ‡

The essays in this book were previously published in the following publications and are reprinted here with thanks (and, in some cases, minor revisions).

Adirondack Life, "Ratbird Overwhelm," July/August 2016; "Adirondacks Inside Out," May/June 2015; "Steep and Difficult of Ascent," July/August 2013; "Sledpacking," January/February 2011; "The Great Derangement," Summer 2014.

Northern Woodlands, "So Gone," Winter 2016.

Seven Days published the pieces that comprise "Seven Lengths of Vermont": "Flyover: The Animal That Contains All Animals," November 2012; "Lake Champlain: Voyage of the Man-Boat," October 2012; "Connecticut River: Paddle Buddy Meets the Actual," September 2012; "Bicycle Touring: The Other Side of the Range," July 2012; "Catamount Trail: Earning Something Hard to Name," March 2012; "Hitchhiking: A World beyond Routine," January 2012; "The Long Trail: A 273-Mile Animal," November 2011.

Vermont Magazine, "Wilderness at Home," May/June 2017; "Seat Mountain," September/October 2016; "Green Ghost Town," July/August 2015; "Frostbiting with Frostbiters," Winter 2015; "Bumping into Life," May/June 2014; "On Track," May/June 2013; "Spandex and Firepower," January/February 2013; "Autumn Snows," November/December 2012; "The Smiles Are Huge," January/February 2011; "A Grebe to Save Our Souls," November/December 2011.

Yankee, "Seeing Is an Art," March/April 2018; "Return to Silver Fields," January/February 2015.

LEATH TONINO, a writer from Vermont, has also worked as a wildlife biologist in Arizona, a blueberry farmer in New Jersey, and a snow shoveler in Antarctica. His essays, reported stories, and interviews appear in magazines such as *Outside, Men's Journal, Orion, Tricycle, Utne Reader,* and *The Sun.* When not at his desk, he roams North America's libraries and wildlands.